THE SECRET OF MEDITATION

HANS-ULRICH
RIEKER

THE SECRET OF
MEDITATION

SAMUEL WEISER INC.
New York

SAMUEL WEISER INC.
734 Broadway, New York 10003

First published 1955
This United States edition 1974

Printed in Great Britain
ISBN 0 877282-45-5

IN GRATEFUL VENERATION
TO MY GURU
THE VENERABLE LAMA ANAGARIKA GOVINDA

CONTENTS

INTRODUCTION

ONE of the most important spiritual factors in all Asiatic religions is known to us only by name: Meditation.

It is mainly because of meditation that the Asiatic puzzles us, or, more precisely: it is because of meditation that the Asiatic has gained a spiritual fluidity which eludes us in our desire for intellectual understanding.

But we should be wrong if we simply gave up because of this difficulty, and made do with what we chose to call "our limit of comprehension". We, too, can obtain similar results, but we have to follow a different path. The psychological basis is the same in both cases; it is only the spiritual traditions which are so different. This is a factor which we must not underestimate.

One of these traditional differences arose out of the different attitudes towards meditation: while the Asiatic does not need meditation to be sugar-coated, we don't even know what is meant by it. When we do have some inkling, it is only of a tiny fraction of this interesting subject: simply of "some sort of intellectual process"—and nothing further.

Whenever we cannot make lucid intellectual statements about the positive results of a process (such as meditation), we remain either disinterested or sceptical and—negative. In this we differ from the Asiatic who is never disinterested, sceptical or negative to such a degree. This fact explains the undeniable advantage of the Asiatic—his much greater tolerance in everything, not only religion.

Oriental studies, within the last fifty years, have gone very deeply into this large domain of Indian philosophy. They have circumscribed it but not plumbed its depths. The core of the subject has only been investigated in recent years; and here rational science must often be silent and content itself with taking second place to practical psychology. Wherever rational science transcended its natural limits, there the results were misleading, and false speculations took place to a most

9

dangerous extent. The whole subject is so subtle that it is better left alone than tackled wrongly. This applies to Asiatic religions in general, especially to Yoga, and very particularly to meditation. Even today we should not have advanced one single step if a few, a very few, had not been determined enough to investigate this subtle spiritual subject by themselves. They were not driven by curiosity but by the recognition that it is not only intellectual discoveries which matter, but that it is in spiritual experiences that the key to the final mystery may be found.

Their results, although based on the data of rational science, nevertheless overshadowed the latter, for they endowed the dead body of intellectual and academic knowledge with a breath of practical activity and confirmation, and thus made it a living reality. Such were: Bhadantācārya Nyānatiloka, the German Buddhist—Prior of Ceylon, the Nestor of the modern Theravāda; Mme David-Neel, the brave French explorer who lived the life of a Tibetan Lama nun for years; Lama Anagarika Govinda, artist, explorer and sage of German origin, one of the leading experts on Buddhist wisdom in general, and all those others who—unknown to academic and literary circles—anonymously followed the path of practical realization and still follow it; Englishmen, Germans, Americans, Russians, Frenchmen, Italians, Scandinavians. All of them stepped beyond the limits of everyday life into another, a higher life—became as one with their Asiatic masters, and although the newspapers do not print it, have given more to the world than the majority of well-paid politicians; it was they who showed the way to our own self. It is in this direction that the peace of the world lies.

Now unfortunately beyond the small number of those who are truly called there are the many who merely think that they are. They, too, would honestly contribute their share to the salvation of souls and the world, and thus we get books which, although perhaps satisfactory from the academic point of view, are nevertheless quite useless, even if they are not completely false. This is a pity, for there are countless people who, thirsting for the path and its realization, absorb every printed word which they think may help them, just as a sponge absorbs water. It is for them that this book is written, for nobody needs help more than those who walk on the razor's edge between error and truth.

It is not taking the wrong path which is the greatest tragedy, but taking that which is *nearly* right. It is the car which lacks "only" the sparking plugs, the house which lacks "only" the door. And harsh but true words: it is half-education which is the most harmful.

Unfortunately, Western knowledge of Asiatic spirituality is more often found in the garb of the beggar, than wearing cap and gown.

As we have said: many books about meditation have been written, and every one of them has its positive and its negative aspects. Most of them approach the problem theoretically. Their authors are either scientists or mystics or both, but they are rarely sober, experienced practitioners. Those authors who are practitioners did not know how to surmount the difficulty that "nothing precise can be said on these matters", and here again, the reader was left confused and disappointed: again he had tried in vain to make some progress and to gain a deeper understanding.

What is the cause of all this? The answer is simple: the authors, however experienced, were no psychologists—they based their writings on their own *experiences*. However, nothing can be *said* about the experiences of meditation—they can only be experienced. This does not mean at all that meditation cannot be taught. Far from it! It can be taught, but it is important to teach it *correctly*, i.e. to adapt it to the psychological needs of the learner.

A further basic mistake of these books is that they employ the psychology of the Asiatic—old texts and traditional ideas of teaching. They forget that we live on an entirely different spiritual and mental plane. We do not wish to debate whether this plane is superior or inferior—it is different, and that is all that matters. We have different obstacles to overcome, we have to contend with different phenomena, have different religious ideas and aims—in short, there is hardly any psychological structure in which we seem to be related to the Asiatic.

Now, if our psychological bases were indeed diametrically opposed, things would be simpler, for then we should have no need to bother at all: for where the causes themselves are incomprehensible we cannot hope to understand the effects. However, basically, all human beings have the same spiritual structure irrespective of nation and race; it is only that age-old customs have modified our structures, and we cannot ignore these modifications if we wish to arrive at the common goal. For this purpose, what is important is not "how it is done" (in fact nothing is "done" at all), but knowing what is useful and advisable, and what is harmful. If this sounds too prosaic, it is nevertheless, good advice.

At the start, old texts will be found of surprisingly little help, although to the experienced they may become a revelation, for these texts, too, are governed by the law that "nothing can be said about things". This fact is confirmed time after time: what we have actually experienced looks completely different from even the most careful theoretical description of it. What is important cannot be said, it can only be understood; and to show that there is a way to this understanding must be, and is, the first consideration in the writing of any book on meditation. Every step beyond this is bound to lead to failure.

A further common mistake is to indicate the right path in the wrong way.

The more blindly we have been taught to accept Christianity, the more sceptical do we become of anything but our own dogmatic beliefs. Concerning the path to meditation, however, our scepticism is fully justified if no clear answer to our *why* is forthcoming. And it is only right to ask why we should choose this particular way. Even if the way should not lead us to the goal, we should be told why this is so and which would be the better path to follow.

If in this book we do not speak about meditation alone, but also about the deeper states which lie beyond it, we do so merely for the sake of completeness. The reader must not entertain any ideas of entering into them without a teacher for he might otherwise come to grief. A lack of seriousness and of thoroughness merely produces the very opposite of all deep experience—prejudice.

These deeper states, or rather their theoretical description, are the ideal breeding ground for prejudice, especially since these psychical phenomena are the rarest of treasures—even in Asia. And yet we need not fear to step beyond theory, for as incredible as this promise seems at this moment, we ourselves may follow this path one day. Here there is no question of abnormal ability, but only of patience.

I have known very learned Buddhist priests who were completely perplexed by the practice of meditation, and I have met illiterate Indian beggars who were masters of it. Thus, I was logically led to pose the question of the relationship between religion and meditation, for the birth of religion represents the crowning of all meditation. Further, I asked myself which "knowledge", if not the intellectual, is decisive. These are problems which, in the course of this book, will be shown to be fundamental.

I have made a thorough study of the practice of meditation of the South Buddhist School of Theravāda, and those of the North Buddhist Mahayana; and the difference (we shall return to this later) is more than one of names: it shows the basic psychological division of the two main groups of people looking for salvation: the introverts and the extroverts.

Above all, we shall try to show to what extent the spiritual methods of Asia can help us. One thing is certain: every attempt to make progress here must fail if we overlook the most basic factor—the spiritual tradition to which all of us—Asiatics and Europeans alike—are more tightly bound than we believe.

In my book *Der Yogi und der Komödiant* (The Yogi and the Comedian) I tried to find the general psychological meeting-ground for both these worlds—I am fully conscious of the inadequacy of so general an attempt. Nevertheless, I stand by my attempt, for it is our—the European's—task to clarify these problems with all the means at our disposal.

In this book I have made a more detailed attempt to provide a practical guide for those who would discover the secrets of their own soul. The book, it is hoped, may also contribute something to practical psychology; for there is nothing in it that cannot be tried by anyone, nothing that cannot be experienced and confirmed.

I believe that I have given the honest seeker (and his number is legion) a means which, while not requiring scientific study, nor involving him in wild mystical speculation, may yet enable him to reach every man's goal: that self-recognition which is the source of all wisdom, and mastery of the problems of life and living.

We shall not discover a new Gospel, any new doctrine of salvation. We shall simply look into our own hearts. Perhaps our objective is even less than that: we shall only recall what we have always known, and what we have forgotten in the struggle for life, because of cares, suffering, pain and avarice; and suddenly, from within ourselves—from our own "self"—there will emerge a new world of wonder. We shall see that it is not a special credo, but all-embracing truth which is lacking in us. And if we are deeply rooted in our own religion—we shall remain so. What we shall gain here is the key to that door which bars the path to our own power.

WHY MEDITATION?

THERE are people who no longer ask, "What is meditation?" Blessed are they! But strangely, not only those who know "meditation" merely by hearsay, but also those who know quite a lot about it (theoretically), keep on asking this question. From this we may learn a very basic fact:

Only those who have experienced it themselves can fully understand the value of meditation!

That may sound discouraging; but we dare not simply dismiss facts because they are discouraging. It is only too natural, for how could we know the value of anything fully, if we haven't tried it ourselves? We can only answer the question "what does a mango taste like?" if we have tasted one ourselves, from our *own experience*. As long as we have not done so, we have to rely on the reports of those who have had that experience, and whose judgment we trust.

Thus somebody might tell us: a mango is sweet like a pear, it is juicy like a peach, it has a smell reminiscent of turpentine, it is soft like a banana, golden like an orange, its skin is tough like thin leather, its kernel is hard and flat and two-thirds the size of the entire fruit, which is oval and as large as a saucer.

This enables us to make an intellectual judgment; and when we actually come to eat a mango, then we can say: yes, quite right, just as it was described. It might have been correct, but the mere description was no substitute for the actual tasting, for only that can tell us if we like mangoes, and how much we like them. Only then do we *truly* know what a mango is. What was described were its *characteristics*, but what was experienced was its *essence*.

Mangoes are not to everyone's taste—nor is meditation. This fact, too, must not be ignored. However positive its results (nourishing and sweet as a mango—to stick to our metaphor), the path is still strenuous: there will be disappointments in unsuccessful attempts and unfulfilled expectations. It is truly a hard and long struggle, but here, as in other things it may be said: "The harder the struggle, the greater is the victory."

The reader may well ask: "Why is the path so long and so hard? Is it not possible that, just for once, the goal might be reached quickly?" This can only be answered noncommittally both with a "Yes" and with a "No". Let us take an habitual smoker as an example, and let us tell him to stop smoking. If this smoker (provided that he *really* is an habitual smoker) from that very moment no longer experiences even the slightest need for a cigarette (or for whatever else he smokes); indeed, when he cannot even understand why he had to smoke at all before, then such a man could gain positive results without any great effort of patience, self-control or time. For—and now we can answer the question "Why Meditation?" more easily—he who can deal with his weaknesses in so masterful a manner either needs no meditation, or has already reached his goal.

The problem, in fact, is not how to suppress small or great weaknesses, but how to leave them by the wayside, how not to *need* them any more. To need them and yet to control them is merely a question of energy, and has nothing to do with higher development. In some cases the total store of energy may be increased—which in itself is not to be scoffed at; in others all the possible repressed complexes are created, which in their turn become the sources of new, and generally greater, problems. Sometimes it is only a small step from "increased energy" to "psychological over-tension".

Why meditation?—or better: what profit can we derive from meditation? If it were simply some new religion, merely some new ritual without any real basis, and thus without any real goal, then it would not only be daring, it would be impudent to renounce our bright world with all its emancipated thought, for the questionable half-darkness of the Asiatic Middle Ages.

Never was humanity more in need of meditation than it is today. In other words: just *because* we live in times of emancipated thought, we must think a little of "ourselves" from time to time, and in our fight to become supermen—even if for only half an hour at a time—we must simply become human. We have almost forgotten how to do this.

It is not true that humanity has become callous and does not desire self-enlightenment any longer. Concerts, theatres, operas, art exhibitions all over the world have scores of visitors, great works of literature are read as much today as at any other time, churches and temples are filled at the usual hours, mountains, seas and forests still move our spirit to its very depths, happy eyes follow the laughter of children, the loveliness of flowers, the grace of animals; and in the eternal "I and you" of simple humanity we love, yearn and suffer as ever.

What has this to do with meditation?—everything! Here it begins, here is its aim: in life. In this pulsating, colourful, passionate life which we are too busy to stop and look at. Those who reproach the Buddha—the greatest teacher of meditation—with being a nihilist, a pessimist, a negativist and other dark things, have misunderstood him so basically that the time and effort which they have spent on studying Buddhism seems utterly wasted. No—Buddhism, on the contrary, is a religion near to life, for it will and must be *experienced* in being *lived*. No easy demand this, but only those who can fulfil it, may venture to judge.

And meditation?—here too, only those can judge who have experienced it, whom it has enriched, who have discovered that this, the strangest phenomenon of all true religions has nothing in common with what we rightly reject as life-negative in goody-goody religious people. Meditation belongs to the innermost core of our beings, and demonstrates the inseparable unity of all life processes and of all true religions.

To the enlightened it shows the great unity of our world with our own essence; truths will appear where none were suspected, for truth is everywhere. To *believe* this is beautiful, but to *experience* it is the highest lot which can befall man.

B

THE INWARD GLANCE

SOMEONE is at an Art Exhibition. As if spellbound he gazes at a masterpiece. Is it the colour, the canvas or the harmony which entrances him? None of these, he will say. Is it the figure or the landscape in the picture? Again he will say no. What then is it? He cannot answer.

We meet him again on the following Sunday. It is a lovely summer's day. He steps from his house as if on winged feet, a book under his arm: *Shakespeare's Sonnets*. Into the beautiful countryside he goes, to sit in the shade of a tree upon a hill, to look far down the river valley into the forest, the billowing fields and the small romantic village.

There he sits—forgotten are his cares, his yesterday, his tomorrow, yes, almost his here and now. Like Faust he would exhort the moment: "Oh do but stay, thou beauteous form." Alas, we must disturb him.

"Why," we ask him, "are you so happily lost in the contemplation of Nature? What is it that holds you entranced? And what was it yesterday when you beheld the Old Master? And the day before when you listened to Beethoven's Ninth Symphony? And what will it be tonight that will hold you prisoner to the radiance of your beloved's dear blue eyes?"

It is not "something on which I can put my finger", he will answer, no "this or that". We must agree with him, for were it the "magic of the thing itself", even the gallery attendant should have been transfixed, the postman walking through the meadow, the usher at the concert hall, and the landlady of his blue-eyed beloved. No, it is within ourselves; it is our heart which opens up because we are willing to have it so, and into our heart flows untold happiness—ours for the asking.

Yet one feels somewhat uneasy about this rather poetic point of view. Happiness isn't just there. Nor unhappiness. For how else can the spell be broken so suddenly, when our friend notices, that while he was lost in the contemplation of the countryside, someone made off with his wallet? Or if on this lovely summer's day a snake should have bitten him? If his beloved had deceived him?

We can be happy anywhere once the inner conditions are satisfied. If we suffer physically or spiritually, heaven itself becomes a hell. He who is famished on a fabulous South Sea island would rather be transplanted into a grey suburban granary, where he would find greater contentment for the moment.

All this is not only convincing, it is a platitude, on which I will waste no more words—all my readers are quite aware of it, anyhow. In theory! Do we think like this in practice too? Strangely enough, not at all!

An untold number of people believe (openly or in secret) that they can escape their suffering. Some evil spirit has forced it upon them, they think, and they try their best to shut it out. And should they manage to change place and circumstances they suddenly notice that hardly anything, nothing at all in fact, has changed:

> *The place is good, and good the new condition,*
> *Yet is the old rogue in his old position.*
> —Wilhelm Busch

Old troubles in a new guise! Sometimes a devastating result! An untold number of emigrants know this only too well.

There are further examples. Who is happier: A satisfied beggar or a dissatisfied king? A healthy artisan or an unhealthy millionaire? A good-humoured tramp or an ill-tempered police superintendent?

Everyone is likely to give the same answer, but had he the choice himself, he would rather be a dissatisfied king than a satisfied beggar, an unhealthy millionaire than a healthy artisan, an ill-tempered police superintendent than a good-humoured tramp.

Strange, isn't it? Why do most men choose what is troublesome, rather than happiness? Because (with some justification) they say:

A good mood, a feeling of happiness may be gone tomorrow. Wealth is more durable. And if I feel dissatisfied, it is easier to gain satisfaction with money—moods change within the space of a second. True, even riches may be lost, but usually not half as quickly as dispositions, moods, transitory happiness. What objections can we have to this?

There are two ways of helping mankind to achieve happiness and satisfaction: either by providing material benefits for all, or by consolidating man's feelings of happiness and satisfaction.

Seneca says: "If you wish to give happiness, do not multiply possessions, but reduce wants."

This is easier said than done; because even if we are convinced that numerous desires together with the impossibility of satisfying them only create suffering and dissatisfaction, the desires themselves, which are the true sources of suffering, are not removed thereby. Yes, even the certain conviction that the desired object is quite worthless does not mean that we cease striving to obtain it.

The reason for this is that while we are certain about *what* we desire, we do not know *why* we desire it. It is not always a practical purpose towards which we strive—often we have the most confused, strange, obscure and inexplicable motives. Certainly when a hungry person begs for a penny in order to buy bread, we need not look for anything obscure; but when Mrs. Miller "absolutely" needs a new dress because she has "absolutely nothing to wear" (her wardrobe is full of dresses) she may do so for a hundred different reasons—simple vanity, the desire to appear rich (that is to say influential), the desire to please an admirer, to put her girl friend in the shade, to show people how many things she can afford, or simply to rekindle her own husband's cooling embers.

To sum up: Man always seeks something which will give him a brief moment of satisfaction; and his psyche will often follow the most tortuous paths to obtain this moment.

Material means must lead to spiritual satisfaction—this law appears to govern our daily lives. Spiritual satisfaction, however, can be produced in the spiritual sphere itself, without the roundabout way of matter and, if we fail to obtain it, it is only because we have no conception of the workings and potentialities of the psyche. Because we blame the lost collarstud and not our own impatience, the rain and not our own lack of resistance, money and not our own desires, because we look for a scapegoat everywhere, we do find it, but not in its real hide-out—in ourselves.

This leads to the well-known attitude: things go badly with me though I am a good man. The fault is with my fellow citizens, with my environment, with God and the Devil, but where the fault *really* lies, there alone (so we think) is goodness, innocence and undeserved suffering.

However, when things go well with me, then apparently I have "deserved" them. In the morning I have given alms to three beggars, helped a blind old man across the street "although I had very little time", and decided to buy my wife a posy. Well, I ask you, doesn't that make me a good man? With a proudly swelling chest we enter our office, and behold! —everything runs more smoothly.

Is it because Heaven has recompensed me for my good deeds?—possibly. Certainly, however, it is because a swelling chest leads to much more positive results than a knitted brow. This is the psychological result of psychological causes. Nor is it always especially difficult and serious things; very often very small causes (or those which we consider to be small) have very large effects. The less we care about causes, the more helplessly are we exposed to their effects.

Thus, when we do not know whence they come, we become the victims of our own bad moods. If we do know their origin, the bad mood may not be dispelled, but we know better "next time".

We have to gather experience, not so much of the world around us, as of ourselves.

"I know myself very well" is an extremely dangerous sentence, for I believe I can say with certainty: there are so few men on this our earth who really know themselves, that they can be counted on the fingers of one hand. The most gigantic task of man is to learn to know and to conquer himself. For then his success will have no limit.

We do not even have an inkling of our capabilities, for good or for evil. Is it not a shame to let so many forces which are incontestably present go by the board, unused? Even though we can hardly succeed in reaching the very limits of our possibilities in the course of a short life, every single step in this direction bears fruit, rich beyond our wildest expectations.

Then what prevents us from knowing and using these potentialities?

Let us take the case of a man who is known to his acquaintances as a most moving orator. Today he has been somewhat upset, and when asked to perform, he regrets "today I am not at my best". Were he a professional artist, legally forced to perform, he would have to "forget" his sorrow and simply have to do his best—just as Pagliacci had to do, even though his beloved had died only a few minutes earlier.

We are too influenced and distracted by sense impressions to free ourselves from them. Were we able to do so, however, and if we looked deep into ourselves instead, we should gather tremendous forces and great potentialities.

If you doubt this, try the following:

It will not be difficult to recall a mistake (if possible of the last few days). You will agree that it will be extremely interesting to know *why* you have made the mistake, and if the reason which you give is the true one.

If the author is right, you should be able to find this out simply by concentrating on the mistake, or on its known causes. Yes, but only if *every* thought is traced back to the mistake for a space of approximately five minutes, and if you think of absolutely nothing else than what you want to know.

Hardly a minute will have passed when your thoughts are somewhere quite different, because suddenly something "came into your mind". If, however, you look at the thought which "came into your mind" in turn, and examine it carefully, just as carefully as the original thought, you will invariably find that it has either a distant, an indirect, or perhaps even a direct relationship with the original thought; or, on the other hand, that it concerns something which "at the moment" appears to be quite irrelevant and trivial. However, you may rest assured that this latter has some important *inner* connection with the thought.

Here now we have one of the most interesting psychological problems: What *really* moves my inner self? What do I *really* desire? What is the origin of my ideas?

The more we concentrate on a fixed thought, the nearer do we psychologically approach the state of sleep, to whose "notions" we are delivered up unconditionally. Today we

hardly need mention that all dreams have a psychological
significance and that they are all capable of saying something
to us.

Dreams give psychological satisfaction to conscious or mis-
placed wishes, and make up for our inadequacies in an immediate or indirect (symbolical) manner. They dominate us
while the will sleeps. If, in the waking state, we concentrate
on an object, chosen of our own *free* will, then those very
thoughts will arise which the dream would have conjured up
at that moment. This may either be the solution of the posed
question, or another matter which, however, interests us more
than the whole question altogether. For, in a condition of concentration, the active Will behaves—as we will see later on
more clearly—almost as in sleep: it becomes weaker than our
instincts which prevent it from rising into consciousness, and
in its stead, strange but pure truth rises to the surface.

The following is an example: Mr. Miller is of the opinion
that it was a mistake to have broken off negotiations with
Smith and Co., for the latter have just concluded a big deal
with Mr. Miller's competitors.

He asks himself: "Have I really broken off the negotiations
only because they asked for too large a discount? Shouldn't I
have come down a little in my price?"

He now concentrates on this question but, after only a
few minutes, he comes to the conclusion that his thoughts
have long passed on to something quite different: they are
suddenly concerned with Dr. Sourman. Quickly back to the
chosen problem!

Again hardly a minute has passed when the question of the
best time for his vacation arises. A third attempt ends with
the sudden idea of going to the office a little earlier today, in
order to buy his wife a birthday present.

"How is it possible," Mr. Miller asks, "that I am so frequently and senselessly disturbed in my important thoughts?
What have these side-issues to do with my important problem?"

Mr. Miller does not realize that the whole problem is only a
side-issue for his unconscious—the "senseless disturbances" are
far more important to it. For actually the situation is as follows:

On the day of his negotiations with Smith and Co., Mr.
Miller had met Dr. Sourman on the way to his office.

"I am just going to call on your wife," the doctor had said; and Mr. Miller had thought of paying a surprise visit to his house to see what the two were up to, because Dr. Sourman was known to be a bit of a Don Juan. Then, however, Mr. Smith had turned up and Mr. Miller had been unable to go home.

Had Smith and Co. agreed to the price, the business would have materialized, and a vacation trip would have been certain—yes, if the truth must be told, even had the deal been concluded at a lower price. But as for the vacation, there is more to it than meets the eye.

Mr. Miller had wanted to spend his holidays in the mountains, but Mrs. Miller had insisted on the seaside, and on the very place that Dr. Sourman was in the habit of frequenting. To let her go there by herself?—"No. I'd rather do without my vacation altogether. But she will only agree to stay at home if we have no money (no other excuse would do), and if the business with Smith and Co. doesn't materialize, then I have no money. As for Dr. Sourman, I'll get him out of the way by buying my wife a beautiful birthday present."

It is for this reason that Mr. Miller had refused to bargain, that the business had not materialized, that he had been able to go home earlier (Dr. Sourman had already left, however) to confess to his wife that the holiday was somewhat uncertain.

Such is Mr. Miller's position, but only we know that, not Mr. Miller himself, who knows nothing about *meditation*. He has simply "forgotten" these things. He thinks it is all due to the pigheadedness of Smith and Co.—meditation doesn't even enter the picture.

On another occasion he is sure to·think: Dr. Sourman is a rogue, and I can't trust my wife.

He forgets that with a little more consideration, his place as victor would have been assured. Yes, even where the holiday was concerned, the friendly but definite word should have been: "We'll go on holiday together!" This would have been the ideal solution. The unconscious knows this, for it made the good suggestion of the birthday present; only consciousness thinks it is so precocious and clever, that it finds ways of even cloaking its own faults and of excusing them. For, although he doesn't admit it, Mr. Miller is a weakling, a hen-pecked husband who would rather lose business than dare to assert himself at home. To admit this, however, is apparently impossible for Mr. Miller; yes, even the smallest step in this direction is cloaked with lies and self-deception, with the high-sounding names: "fate", "misfortune", "bad luck" or, even worse, "pre-destination". Let this be an example to millions.

"Aha," the psychologist will now say, "self-analysis!" He is right. The only difference lies in the fact that psycho-analysis uncovers past faults, whereas meditation creates its own psychological basis for action. In other words, not therapy but prophylaxis, if we must give it a name. Prophylaxis, however, against germs for which no vaccines exist: error, false conclusion, yes, even that germ which Dr. Hiob Praetorius searched for in vain:

The germ of human stupidity!

That is the answer to the question: "What is meditation?"

Certainly an unassuming word for a most important matter; but it would be very stupid to condemn something only because we have not yet tried it out sufficiently, and because we suspect that the hydrogen bomb is the height of all human endeavour.

The simple, let it be said, is never quite as simple as the difficult. The atom bomb has now been invented, not so the fountain-pen that never leaks. We have preventive means against smallpox, not, however, against the common cold. And with all this, the leaky fountain-pen gives us more trouble than the undivided atom, the common cold more bother than smallpox.

Similarly, we can cure the most complicated psycho-pathological diseases, while we are rather helpless in the psychopathology of everyday life, and yet we have the ways and means not only of healing the spiritual common cold, but even of preventing it. Commendable though it be not to attach too great a significance to error, to false conclusion, to prejudice and stupidity, and just to accept them as such (if sometimes with a small sigh), it would do us good to realize that the true suffering of the world, too, is due to error, to false conclusion, to prejudice, and to stupidity. Or could anybody honestly contend that wars had any other causes?

WHAT IS MEDITATION?

"Very well," says Mr. Miller, "but I am no Indian Yogi. I just can't do it. I lack the peace of mind for it. Perhaps the Indian Yogis have nothing better to do. We city people live under different conditions."

Mr. Miller is absolutely right: we city people do live under conditions which differ greatly from those of the sages who for years on end live in the jungle and in "perfect meditation". If we ignore this we shall commit error upon error, and this is just why this book has been written: for Mr. Miller, not for the jungle dweller. Meditation is meditation for Mr. Miller just as it is for the Yogi, but the path to it is different, for each of them has to overcome different obstacles. And should the one proceed from the spiritual basis of the other, he is bound to fail, for our path to meditation is determined by our inner make-up.

The Buddhist monk is forbidden to go to the theatre, to exhibitions, etc. This is understandable, for most of these monks are simple natives, to whom such impressions might become soul-shaking experiences, simply because they lack the intellectual toughness to keep their souls untouched by such experiences.

We see the theatre "through different eyes". It may even soothe our troubled spirits. We can keep our distance from sense impressions and yet recognize their spiritual essence.

In many ways, however, the native monk is better off than we are, for his obstacles and also his problems are not nearly as great as ours. If he were confronted with new facts he would have to digest them first—we, however, are born into them. Our disadvantage is that we have manifold desires and our advantage is that we know most of them so "well" that our attitude towards them is quite ingrained. Thus, for instance, a capital city of another country is not "as new" to us as it would be to a jungle-dweller who would be overwhelmed not only by the "strange environment" but even more so, by the many little attractions, such as radios, cars, trams, lifts, elevators, etc. As long as the pious jungle-dweller knows nothing of these things and their attractions, there is little to disturb his pious ways of living. Those of us, however, who have tasted of the numerous attractions of our world, and who have *then* outgrown them of our own free will, have probably gone farther along the road to completion.

A Ceylonese monk once said to me:

"I do not know the things of your world; but I believe that I should have to leave my order if I did get to know them, for I should succumb to that world. I can imagine it. I cannot know it. In any case I am afraid of it, but most of all, I fear my own weakness." A wise man indeed!

Here we have the difference between Mr. Miller and the jungle-dweller. It makes no difference whether the attractions are great or small, simple or complicated, natural or artificial. The only thing that matters is the fact that they *are* attractions, i.e. that we have to come to terms with environmental influences, whether these influences are a coconut or a helping of crayfish mayonnaise.

Mr. Miller toys with the idea of a new car, the Yogi with that of a new rice-bowl; but for both, the acquisition is no absolute necessity—the attraction is the same, the considerations are also the same, yes, even the percentage of what has to be invested in the purchase is the same. Why shouldn't both of them attack their desires in the same way? Provided, naturally, that they need attacking in so far as the fulfilment of the wish would be a disadvantage.

Both of them have only three ways of doing this:

1. The wish is displaced. That is the usual way and also the simplest. But a displaced wish is by no means destroyed, just as an undiscovered theft does not cease to be a theft simply because it is undiscovered. No: what has happened has happened—nothing can be changed in it. A deep-rooted wish can only be removed by its fulfilment.

2. The wish is overcome, when it is not deep-rooted, i.e. when it has not become a psychological obsession.

Wishes of the moment can change their object: psychologically they remain the same wishes, only their material form changes. This happens when a jilted lover, toying with the idea of suicide today, nevertheless marries another three weeks later; when the wife who wants a fur coat is fully satisfied with a diamond ring, and so on.

People who constantly find new disguises for their desires can easily lie to themselves. They transform the most primitive wishes into such ideal objects that they easily become heroes both to themselves and to those near them. Hitler, whose personal ambitions became transformed into the apparent wish "to free the Fatherland", is a typical example of this.

No less great is the danger when these masked strivings are found in the religious sphere, and when the "wish to renounce" becomes a new passionate desire.

The Buddha spoke wisely when he said:

"Not only *evil* passions are to be overcome, but *good* passions as well; for *all* passions are a hindrance."

Surely a good deed is no less good because it was done after careful reflection? "Passionate impulses" are often regretted when passion has given way to "objective consideration"—and a good deed which is regretted had better been left undone.

3. There remains the third possibility: meditation.

How does this work?

Simply in that the wish is prevented from becoming a psychological obsession. It is, however, not the wish itself that is influenced, but the spiritual sphere in which the wish is rooted. There is a great difference between the wishes of a fool and those of a sage.

Influencing the wish *itself* means displacing it; attacking its *content* could easily "transform" it; to recognize and to cultivate the ground on which the wish grows, however, means to affect the spiritual momentum of the wish. Only this can have fruitful results, and must be attempted.

Let us compare a stupid Mr. Miller with an intelligent Mr. Miller:

Every time he takes a walk, stupid Mr. Miller will be cross, will get sore feet (the result of his displaced complexes), will curse at every bus and finally at every car driver, by changing his unfulfilled "car desire" into the apparently most noble wish of "safeguarding the pedestrian from the madness of car drivers!" He projects his own inadequacies, his own stupidity, on to the objects of his environment, and thus his mania is complete.

On the other hand, wise Mr. Miller has been able to recognize and to de-limit the realm of his wish within him by meditation. He knows: "I desire. In me there is a wish. This wish is responsible for my attitude towards my environment, the environment itself, however, has nothing to do with it." Thus he does not consider his walking a result of an unfulfilled desire, but a natural fact. The bus will not make him cross, for how can it help the fact that Mr. Miller does not possess a car? He will not hate the lucky car owner, but at worst he will consider him an incentive to renewed and greater activity.

To us outsiders these thought processes seem to be so logical and natural that we hardly understand stupid Mr. Miller. But let us beware—as long as we consider Mr. Miller's situation without bias, it is easy to see what is right and to suggest it. It is always easy to give good advice—it is much more difficult, however, to follow it oneself.

Strangely, we are never governed by our intellectual powers, but rather by the experience which life has given us. This world of experience, however, does not take the intellectual measure of good or evil, for otherwise there would only be wise and good people, and not the large number of those who would gladly "do good", but cannot; who cannot because they do not know how to use their own experiences over and above their intellectual understanding (through meditation), and cannot follow that path which is better both for them and for those near and dear to them—the path which would give them happiness. It is difficult to convince those of the practical value of meditation who are absolutely certain that only their environment is to blame for their misfortune—never they themselves. Meditation will not create the Golden Calf, nor an inexhaustible bank account; it can, however, change the face of the world because the face of the world is always that which we give it.

If we have won the Irish Sweep, a rainy autumn day will look quite different from what it does when the bailiff knocks at our door, yet the weather is the same in both cases.

Meditation changes us from poor victims into active

creators. It makes us aware of hitherto undiscovered powers within us. It gives us peace and raises us above despair because there are places inside us which lack of peace, anxiety and despair cannot reach, and which allow us to survey the world and life, as we would a rugged landscape from the soft upholstery of an aeroplane.

Meditation is homoeopathic medicine to be taken once or twice daily. Nothing more. Once or twice daily we must "collect" ourselves, we must bethink ourselves, become human, and cease being beasts of burden.

What is beautiful during a holiday may be ours constantly. And why not? It costs no money, indeed, in the long run it can even bring wealth, for self-possession, mastery of situations, strength of nerve and reflection have never made any man a loser.

"I cannot do it", is a flat lie, a poor excuse for our own shiftlessness.

Admittedly, it is not easy to expect patience, great patience, in an era in which the penny is put in the slot above, and the result is expected below; but he who has no patience must learn it, and he who has it—"blessed man"—already has the foundations of success within him. Meditation is the surest way to healthy success in life. It is not, as half-educated laymen would have it, a somersault into self-forgetting hallucinations, a flight from the cares of the world into a negative dream condition, a mystical pipe-dream. On the contrary!

Meditation is a systematic path to clear self-recognition, it is the knowledge that the trouble with the world stems from within us and is not a catastrophic something which governs us from without. No intoxication—but on the contrary an awakening from the intoxication of misguided habits to the absolute ownership of what we ourselves have fashioned and which now threatens to become our master: the world.

We have two kinds of possessions: material and spiritual, that is, the perishable and imperishable, the endangered and the safe.

Today we ought to be a little more sceptical of material possessions; we have seen in our bomb-ruined cities those who were once the richest and happiest—who overnight became beggars—and are now extremely wretched; they have nothing but the memory of a past, forever gone, and only emptiness and despair before them.

Yet we also know of those who, because of their unbreakable spirit, were thrown behind barbed wire and martyred, those who smiled even in death and who neither cursed nor despaired. It was they who had a greater, a spiritual, possession which could not be touched by suffering or despair—they who felt no pain because they had known what it is to possess happiness.

Certainly, only a few will reach this goal. The path to it is long and difficult. But should we not at least try to clarify our attitudes towards material and spiritual possessions? After all, having the one does not mean renouncing the other; yet some imperishable possessions are surely the most certain assets, if one day—perhaps for the third time in this century—we should again face destruction.

If then, we have imperishable spiritual possessions, indestructible spiritual powers, and if in the face of the most extreme danger, we are at peace within ourselves, surely this is no pessimism, but on the contrary, an absolute "Yea" saying to life. For "living" does not mean that we enjoy the world till all passion is spent, but rather that we stand at the helm, and know that we are masters of our fate and not its slave—master of our joys and master of our sorrows.

For wherever there is joy, there will be sorrow also. It is up to us whether our sufferings break us or make us. It is up to us, and it lies within us. We have only to find the path.

THE PATH TO MEDITATION

IT sounds easy when we are told that what is mainly required in meditation is an ability to concentrate. "Concentrate!" is the beginning of all well-meaning introductions to the subject. But even at this early stage the expectant reader is wont to hesitate, for he does not know how to set about it.

True, he can well imagine *what* concentration is, but he himself has not *experienced* it; since in our world of ever-changing fashions, the demand for concentration is apparently insignificant. Understanding is made so easy for us that we are satisfied with intellectual superficialities, because "it's good enough for everyday life".

From time to time, however, concentration becomes an urgent spiritual necessity, and so we go to the cinema or to the theatre, possibly in order to concentrate, but not as we should do—on ourselves, *in* ourselves, but *away from* ourselves on something else. Once the performance is over, we often feel as if we had just awakened on the day of a hopeless law-case: from the happy distraction of our dreams to our usual dull cares.

This concentration—on *self-forgetting* is much sought for and easily obtained. Yes, we need it, as the addict needs his drug. But if we speak of concentration on the *self*, then to most it is a strange concept in a foreign tongue, or at best a theoretical abstraction. We are sceptical because we suspect that there is some religious speculation behind it all, and because of our misconceptions we dislike the whole idea.

It is by no means our wish to denigrate the enjoyment of art. Concentration in the theatre, the concert, while gazing at a work of art, in the contemplation of Nature, is not quite as *self-forgetting* as it looks.

In it, we become victims of a force, stronger than the grey world around us. A chord is struck within us, one that may lie dormant during our care-worn everyday lives; and every time that we emerge from this kind of concentration we become a little strengthened and enriched.

How could the beautiful gladden us if it were not within us in the first place? We only need the *means* to awaken the response in our soul. Yet we no longer know how, we have not learnt it, or perhaps we have mis-learnt it.

We are not free, simply because we are dependent on external *stimuli*, and if they are lacking, then happiness seems to be lacking also. Our spiritual strings are muted as long as no outer vibration makes them resonate.

We have, however, only ourselves to blame for this short-coming. Why is our epoch less spiritual than that of our fore-fathers? Why is wisdom more often found in the hermit's cave than in the flat of the intellectual?—because our "mass soul" has become too lazy to find happiness in itself. We no longer even know what is meant by "happiness *per se*", for with every other care, this, too, has been taken off our shoulders. If we want to "feel well" or happy, we must have "something" which "makes" us happy and this something we call our "need". But was there no satisfaction in those times in which our "needs" were unknown? The chances are that there was a great deal more of it.

This is the curse of our age; first we create new needs, and then we try to satisfy them in the most exciting way. That is the position; yet it is not wise to rebel against this historical development—it must be mastered. It is not he who succumbs who is the master, but he who controls his needs.

Do we really need our "necessities"? We might do well to look at this question a little more closely. To anticipate: the answer to this question will not be "all your requirements are vain and useless! Renounce them and become saved!" No, matters are not quite so simple, and those who act too quickly here will have to pay heavily for it later on.

Let us look at it purely theoretically: what do we *really* need? A look at our room alone will give us the answer.

Let us remove just a few of the frightening number of necessities (please, not the most unimportant, that will do later, but the most important, such as books are for the intel-lectual). What would happen? Would life cease to be worth living? Would we be near suicide? An intellectual, for instance, who would value the ownership of books as much as life itself, only proves how little he has absorbed from them—how very

c

much he depends on the knowledge of others. Everybody can look up references; but true knowledge is power. Let us concentrate on the thought that through a catastrophe we might be robbed of all those things which have become our necessities, and let us investigate how much of the loss is a *true* loss, i.e. how far it can affect us within, or rather how much it could change us, for that is the decisive question. Catastrophes usually follow the law of supply and demand, and no one can say with certainty that he might not have to make such a decision at any moment.

Owing to the events of the last decade, a great part of humanity is no longer so averse to discussing this question. It knows that the result may be very positive, for as experience has shown, we can more easily do without our "necessities" when we *must* do without them. Every one of us will have to confront this "*must*" once in his lifetime at least—at the moment of his final leave-taking.

The more deeply we enter into the question of ownership and loss, the more clearly a second question will emerge: what is man's dearest possession on earth? Luther says: "Let them take our body, goods, honour, child and wife . . ." Those are our dearest possessions! Who could have put it better than this master of words?

Here we have everything that is our "necessity", everything that we really or apparently "need for life". Which of these, however, cannot be lost? Which does not daily and hourly become a source of sorrow? Only a fool will die of sorrow for his lost possessions; the wise man's possessions, however, are imperishable.

Nothing but meditation can help us here. Abstract speculations about the world to come are irrelevant; for it is impudent to ask for gods so long as human problems are still unsolved. After all, which problems are more urgent than those concerning "life, goods, honour, child and wife"? Not even that of the soul! Those who think otherwise are thereby in no better position to solve it, they must tackle the problems of ownership first.

Who will go to church when his house is burning?

The path to meditation requires that our relationship to our own body, to our own possessions, to our own honour and family must first be resolved. Not by striving to loosen the bonds which tie us to these concepts, but through the conviction that the many sorrows which our possessions bring with them are an unnecessary waste of energy; and that through a positive feeling of happiness, through *natural* self-consciousness, through the recognition of our own strength we can achieve incomparably greater things. If we can do this, then we shall find that there are hardly any limits to our higher development; and that even the slightest progress in this direction may bear the richest fruits.

However, even so small a step involves something rather unpleasant: the breaking of our daily ritual.

Those who believe that habits are weaknesses can be much more easily persuaded. Meditation is a cultivated weakness, because it is based on doing nothing, but it has very positive results.

The Asiatic—we may "reproach" him with it—is inclined to doing nothing. On the streets of the Orient he can be seen squatting lazily on his heels, arms folded over his knees; the work by which he must earn his daily bread may be done today, tomorrow, or perhaps next week. It doesn't matter.

We certainly don't like this state of affairs, and from our point of view it is indubitably undesirable. The sage, however, is guided by just this psychology. And indeed: what wisdom is deeper than that of the East? Do not all religions originate in the East? And which religion, which philosophy, teaches unseemly haste?

Let us say it all in a few words: It is to the Asiatic's knack of doing nothing at all from time to time that humanity is indebted for its greatest spiritual treasures.

There are people who always have to be doing something, and others who never have to do anything. Both are to be condemned as extremes.

Let us be honest: when, during the course of the day do we have ten minutes to ourselves? And not in the sense of *self-forgetting*, but in that of self-reflection!

We should not find it too difficult to rise ten minutes earlier and to "brood" between washing and breakfast; nor should we be too badly affected if we should prolong the day by a further ten minutes to survey the last twenty-four hours, shortly before going to bed. These twenty minutes are not stolen from anybody, do not mean any work, rather are they a salutary form of laziness; they require no effort, neither spiritual nor physical; and the result—as we have said so many times—can only be positive.

By now some of my readers will probably have decided to have a "try", for God knows, meditation has been painted in the most beautiful colours. They will have decided to "try it", and to give it up again if they cannot make a success of it.

If they think like that, they had better not begin at all!

Note the following law: meditation only begins to be successful when we no longer expect it to be so—when it has become a habit.

The governing factor of the whole of meditation is that guiding star of all endurance, of all ambition and of all success in life: patience.

If, for instance, we have decided to learn a language, then, too, we must be patient and persevering; yet even after the first lesson we shall know at least some words of the new language, and that, too, is a clearly demonstrable "success".

Not so in meditation. In vain shall we look for success after the first attempt. Even after a month we shall notice nothing that could significantly be called progress or success. This is discouraging, isn't it?

Indeed, it would not only be *useless* to expect success, it would be *harmful*. Every minute of meditation in which we wait for some mystical event, for a "voice" or a "vision", is time lost.

"Stop!" somebody who knows better will say, "I have often read that it is possible to hear voices and see visions in deep meditation."

My dear friend, do you know the meaning of "deep meditation?" Do you know that it is often preceded by many, many years of patient and persevering exercises? And that the "voices" are no voices, and the "visions" no visions, no pictures? That we cannot *expect* any of these things, because they are entirely different from what we imagine them to be? That what we hope for does not even exist in the form we expect it to have? That a *true* "voice", a *true* "vision" should shake us so deeply and to our very core, that we must first be ripe

THE PATH TO MEDITATION

and armed for such a phenomenon? Alas, my friends, this only applies to the fewest of us, for Nature proceeds in slow stages.

Inner ripening takes place just as unobtrusively and organically as an outer one; and yet, we never expect exceptions in the outer processes.

What should we say if the cherry tree in front of our window were to bud on the first of January, to bloom on the third, to carry leaves on the fifth and flowers on the seventh? Nobody expects this to happen, and yet the physical process of maturing is much quicker than the psychological or spiritual!

What a long, arduous path it was for each of us to attain what little spiritual maturity we have! We have grown organically and never expected an inorganic acceleration of the process. It would have been senseless anyway, for what idea could we have formed of the suffering, the knowledge and the wisdom in store for us when we were but young children! We wanted to be "grown up" certainly; but that was nothing more than some vague idea. And while we were waiting (when shall I finally grow up?) time seemed to be infinite. And the waiting was never successful, for by being "grown-up" we understood nothing but "being big". What it really meant, we neither knew nor suspected, nor were we capable of doing so.

In meditation it is just the same—exactly the same. Trifle with it as you may, the fact remains unchanged—it is a process of spiritual development which matures according to plan and can never be accelerated by force, impatience or anticipation.

Only Nature can help here: those who are patient, who though disappointed and impatient, do not stop the exercise, will one day forget that (only too natural) time of waiting. The exercise will have become a daily habit.

And after a year, should we secretly take stock of our inner forces, we shall have a proud feeling of happiness, for we shall suddenly know:

"Yes, during the last year I have gained something which has become an integral part of my nature—a power which others do not possess, an ability which is greater than that of others."

The second year will take its course quietly, more clearly and more steeply, for then we shall know what is important. We shall have become wiser, more real.

As everywhere, here too, it is only the beginning which is difficult, but here even more so, for nothing in the world demands greater patience than inner development through meditation.

All the other thorns and difficulties which may still appear on this path, and which usually do, will be dealt with in the course of this book as fully as possible. With the necessary goodwill we can easily surmount them.

Let us recapitulate briefly:

The true path to meditation is determined by the following factors:

1. The *conviction* that it is necessary to clear up our inner attitudes:

(*a*) to possessions and to the family
(*b*) to our own Ego ("What sort of a man am I really?")
(*c*) to the "eternal".

2. The *decision* to act from this conviction, i.e. to tackle the spiritual solution of these three questions in a systematic manner. This means we must gain a deeper insight (self-enlightenment) in the form of spiritual development.

Are these all the axioms? Can we begin with meditation now? Let us be patient a little longer, there are still one or two things to be said—we want to clear away as many difficulties as possible.

Nobody will deny that over and above the numerous cares and difficulties of everyday life, a great many of our irritations are due to ourselves.

How were things with Mr. Miller yesterday?—He came into the office (on top of all his other troubles he had wet feet), and he noticed that Miss Nielson had again arrived ten minutes late. He had tolerated this for too long! He had stood enough of her nonsense! Now his patience was at an end! He foamed, he roared. Miss Nielson cried—there, now he had stitches in his heart again! Well, well, the day had started beautifully once more.

And when he came home in the evening, his bickering about the over-salted soup was just a shade too violent.

All this happened yesterday. But let us erase this day from the life of Mr. Miller, and let him re-experience all the same once more, but with this difference: the thought of getting excited will not even enter his head.

"Miss Nielson," he said, "I must warn you! You know I am a very tolerant man at heart, but I want to tell you quite frankly that if you ever come late again, I am afraid I shall have to give you notice. I really mean this, and if you do not believe me, you will have to see for yourself. Well, and now let's get down to work."

Miss Nielson will not cry, there will be no stitches in the heart, and the letter of demand will not be so insulting as to lead to a libel case. The day—in spite of the rain—will be more harmonious, and logic will tell him that the soup will not lose any of its salt by his being cross. And after all, it was not deliberately over-salted by Mrs. Miller.

That evening's meditation will be one more piece successfully fitted into the jigsaw puzzle of his greater development. This would certainly not have taken place in the first case, for rage, irritation, excitement, anger and nervousness are the enemies of all inner harmony.

True, people are often inclined to make things difficult for us, but when we are masters of the situation, of our words and deeds, we not only benefit, but we become terribly proud of having been so "strong", that we shall find it very much easier to control ourselves in future.

To suppress rage is wrong—what we should do is not to let it arise in the first place, for nothing is bad enough to warrant our anger.

The Chinese call lack of control a "loss of face". This is the most embarrassing thing that could happen to anyone, for in rage man is animal rather than human, and "righteous anger" is nothing but a poor excuse.

There are a thousand reasons against rage, and not a single one in its favour.

Those who cannot control themselves at all will find the best and most natural remedy in meditation (on those days when they are peaceful). Their path may be a little longer than that of their fellow-men, for meditation in their case, must first provide an inner balance. Once this is reached—and it is reached very soon—many other positive things will have been attained simultaneously. Only—we must know what we want.

It must be added that *temperament* can be a very fine thing, and that it has absolutely nothing in common with lack of control, although this lack is often wrongly and euphemistically described as temperament.

To repeat: Do not suppress your rage, do not let it devour you, when in fact you want to jump out of your skin, but don't get into a "state" in the first place (for that is lack of control), don't let your tongue run away with you and thus produce even greater anger. For a situation is just what you choose to make of it, and a reasoned word is surely more effective than a wild one.

This gives us a third factor in our preparation for meditation: the guarding of our tongues which are a known source, firstly of our own, and secondly, of other people's rages.

Surely we need not stress that this applies even more strongly to our actions, which should never become outlets for suppressed insults.

In Asia there are two wonderful sayings. One is the Buddha's:

> *If hatred you oppose with fury,*
> *Nor war nor strife will cease.*
> *Forgiveness ends all wrath and envy!*
> *And leads you to eternal peace.*
>
> (Dhammapada 5)

The other is attributed to Confucius:

> *What you would not have done to you*
> *You must not unto others do!*

Mr. Miller pipes up:

"I know what you want to say," he grunts; "you want me to think and act according to these quietistic principles. Very well, but would you please tell me—after all I have a responsible job—am I to take everything lying down? People would just lead me a dance if I let them do as they pleased."

Dear Mr. Miller, what a lame excuse!

Let me tell you something about my own happy days at school in the hope that it might give you some food for thought:

We had two teachers. One we called Jackie and the other

Bill. Not because we were disrespectful or provocative, but because it was the traditional thing to do, and for schoolboys traditions are sacrosanct.

Jackie and Bill were as different as chalk and cheese. Both were of mature years, and both masters of their subject; but whereas one had a vicious temper and flew off the handle at the slightest provocation, the other was a paragon of self-control.

I can still see them now—Jackie the enraged, gesticulating, screaming bundle of nerves; Bill—always smiling, always aware of what he was doing, of what he said and wanted.

Now, Mr. Miller, today you are just like Jackie. Wouldn't you rather model yourself on Bill?

We always looked forward to our lessons with Jackie, because we enjoyed teasing him (youth will be cruel) and seeing him in one of his rages. For his rages used to amuse and to stimulate us, but never really frightened us, for a man who lacks control is never feared, but only pitied. We looked forward to Bill, too, because we enjoyed his personality, more or less instinctively. It is always a true joy to meet a real personality. I cannot remember a single case in which we dared to play a prank which annoyed rather than amused him.

The whole school played the fool with Jackie, and he nearly had an apoplectic fit. Bill simply admonished—and everyone was terribly embarrassed not to have thought of it himself.

For six years he was my teacher, and not once did I see him loose his temper. But we learnt a great deal in his lessons, nonetheless. Or is it just because of this?

What do you think, Mr. Miller?

ASSUMPTIONS FOR SUCCESSFUL MEDITATION

THERE are two factors which inhibit meditation—those from without, and those from within ourselves. The external factors, however, are not nearly as decisive as the internal ones.

If the look of anything disturbs me, I can simply close my eyes; if, however, I am nervous—what shall I do then? If I am irritated by a noise I can close my ears, but if I have worries, how can these be overcome?

We shall devote the next chapter to the question of suitable external conditions. In this chapter, however, we shall discuss inner inhibitions and how to fight them.

Let us begin with the most elementary third of our organism —the body. This is very important, for physical inhibitions have spiritual and psychological results, just as psychological inhibitions have physical and spiritual results. If any one of them is mitigated, then it is easier for the others to be mitigated as well, and this can only be to our advantage. Because of this we consciously strive towards development, physically through sport, etc., psychologically through schooling, and spiritually through the influence of the beautiful (art, etc.).

Unfortunately, we must accept the fact that the fight for spiritual development is rather prosaic—simple and free of all those mysterious Yoga rites which the sensation-hungry Occidental expects of the practising Yogi, in fact of almost every Asiatic. However, there is some cause for rejoicing, for in the first place we shall thus obtain a true picture of those "wonder men", secondly things will be much easier for us than we might have feared, and thirdly we ourselves shall be able to attain within only a few years, what we can only admire from afar today.

Let us begin with a motto:

"The greater our hurry, the longer the way; the greater our patience, the sooner we reach the goal."

42

Our first task is to take stock of our spiritual state in order to know which path must be ours.

For this we must choose a solitary and peaceful evening. Both telephone and radio are switched off. No visitors are expected. The rest of the family is at the cinema, and we are not so tired that sleep is uppermost in our minds.

We take off our shoes, loosen our belt, collar and everything that is too tight, and removing even the smallest danger of being disturbed, we lie on our back on the couch. Head not too high and not too low—body as flat as possible, legs uncrossed, arms stretched freely along the body, fingers (equally freely) stretched out. For a few seconds we try to make ourselves as comfortable as possible, and then we remain motionless. Eyes closed if there is no danger of falling asleep. Finally, we take mental stock of our whole body, from the top of our head to the soles of our feet and to the tips of our fingers, and consciously, but without any movement, we relax all those muscles which are still taut.

Thus—so we have decided—we shall stay for five minutes. (Before starting we look at the clock, but in this position no clock must be in our line of vision. Please note this!)

"Five minutes" means a space of time which appears to us to be five minutes; and "thus to stay" means not moving the smallest muscle, the little finger, the itching nose—nothing at all. What you do with your thoughts does not yet matter. All this may be easy for some, more difficult for others, and many will have breathing difficulties after only one minute. An eye will suddenly begin to itch, or the nose perhaps, or a "fly" may settle on our hand (although in fact there is no fly), fleas, mosquitoes and other insects may suddenly appear in great numbers and immobility may become a horrible torture.

We give up, cursing a little, or perhaps quite a lot, and if we think that we had endured it for five minutes, we shall see to our disappointment that hardly half the time had passed.

As we said, this is what happens to some—to those whose nerves are so bad that this kind of treatment may well be a question of life and death. But let no one despair, for every beginning is difficult. Those who can easily stay the five minutes, without any appearance of nervousness, will forgive us if we ask them to be a little patient and to allow us to deal with their more unfortunate brother first. After all, this is only a test to decide the kind and the duration of our initial training.

First of all we shall decide to do this exercise daily—once a day will be quite sufficient. We shall not try to establish any records—to be doing the exercise from afternoon to midnight by next Sunday—but shall rather set a limit of about five minutes. If, after two minutes, we become nervous, we shall try it for just a little longer—sometimes nervousness ceases by itself. If, however, after another half a minute it has still not gone, then we must stop the exercise. If we have continued for what we think is five minutes, we must stop, for it is not the time which is important, but how we have used our five minutes. If everything is easy, but the five minutes are regularly overestimated, then this is proof that although our nerves are intact, we are still victims of an unhealthy impatience which must be conquered.

But don't let us attribute too much importance to time. We must give up thinking of time during the exercise; and one day (in most cases within a week), we shall know the right time automatically and break off the exercise almost to the second. Not because we can "estimate" better, but simply because we just *know*. These five minutes begin to matter only when they are "fulfilled"—that is, only when we can pass them without difficulty, without changing the position of even one finger, without the slightest wish to scratch anywhere, without feeling the slightest bit uncomfortable, etc. We must be able to break off the exercise at will and without *having to* do so. Thereafter we shall automatically prolong the time.

Normally this is possible after only one week, but the extension is only a small one—one minute—in other words, six minutes now.

Here we have a disappointment in store for those who, from the very beginning, managed to pass the whole five minutes as if in play, and who even managed to estimate the time of ending accurately. They, too, must abide by the same rules, must not exceed five minutes during the first week and only prolong the exercise by one minute in the second week. There are at least two reasons why they are not going to be rewarded by a "better exercise", but these need not concern

them overmuch—we do not want to be burdened with psychological questions more than is absolutely necessary. It is
essential that they follow the same path, and they must just
accept this.

For the exercises the following particulars should also be
known, some of which will be dealt with in greater detail
later on: it is unnecessary to do the exercise more than once a
day—a second exercise on the same day is a waste of time.
Further, the exercise is best done at the same time of day and
in the same place.

The exercise is useless if it is done while family life continues
in the same room. I have heard of a man who did his exercises
on the tiles of the bath-room floor because his living conditions
left him no other choice. A blanket and a cushion were all he
took with him when he disappeared each evening.

If, at this stage when we are merely making preparations
for "true" meditation, the psychological aspect of the matter
is not very important, it is nevertheless advisable that during
the time of these basic exercises we should be reasonably free
spiritually and mentally, and not brood over those things
which have worried us throughout the whole day. We must
decide to erase these minutes from the hustle and bustle of
daily life. This is done by redirecting our thoughts. Please
note: this is not essential, but it is useful to start with what
will become an absolute necessity later on. If possible, we should
avoid actively preoccupying ourselves with our daily cares, for
this simply increases our nervousness. We, therefore, think of
things which present no problem—a picture, a flower, a landscape, in short, something soothing and beautiful. These
thoughts must not be forced, must not be dictated. We wish
to recuperate and this cannot be done by force.

We can even think of "nothing at all" if we have a knack
for it, only not of oppressive and problematical things. Thus
the minutes will pass. Now it is time to stop the exercise.

That does not mean that we jump up quickly and show
how much strength we have gained. The end of the exercise
is marked by a deep breath. This must be remembered. First
the fingers are stretched, then the shoulders, and now the
exercise is finished. What happens after that does not concern
me.

It is obvious that all this cannot really be called meditation. It is merely meant to prepare the ground for it—and the more civilized and cultured we are, i.e. the more manifold our inner life is, the more such preparation is needed. By means of these exercises we shall get a better grip on ourselves, and meditation proper will become considerably easier if we have had some previous successes.

For this reason it is very difficult to say exactly how long these preparatory exercises must be continued. We can merely generalize by saying that it is never advisable to relinquish them before we have been able to master the exercise without difficulty for thirty minutes.

And what precisely is the meaning of "mastered"?

First we must lose our nervousness, and we usually manage to do so, if not entirely and absolutely, at least during the exercises themselves. This is more useful psychologically than one would imagine.

Secondly, we obtain a better time sense. That in itself is no great gain either, and for the time being it will also only be noticed during the exercises. This, too, has a certain psychological value which—in another form and in another place—will be noticed to our advantage.

Thirdly, we shall have the indirect result of the first two. This seldom makes its appearance before the end of six months, and is a feeling that we no longer have a body. We shall not discuss this here, as it belongs to meditation proper, and after all, we want to proceed systematically.

If you compare what we have just said with what we said previously, you will be very surprised; first, you were warned not to expect any success at all because that would only be possible after many long years, and now you are told of very great successes at this early stage—after some weeks, even before the beginning of meditation proper. What does this mean?

Well, "success" here is, in fact, not success at all compared with our goal. True, it is success in the ordinary sense of the word, but only because those very handicaps which we are trying to remove during these weeks of preparatory exercises have depressed us poor city birds below the level of the average healthy human being—and that must be remedied before we can climb higher. If this enables us to rise considerably above our average fellow-men, it does not speak well for our times.

Thus, there is no hurry to change from the preparatory exercises to meditation proper; in fact, it is not even correct to speak of a "change". The ideal case is one of sliding over— but of this later. We should be in no hurry at all, for after all, having managed without meditation for so long, why should we wish to build Rome in a day? We should not be afraid of devoting a whole year to these preparations. When it is before us it seems an age—when behind us, it seems to have flown.

This then is the fight against physical inhibitions.

You may think what you will: that we consider our body so inferior that we do not deem it important enough to fight its inhibitions during meditation proper (for in it only psychological inhibitions proper will be attacked); but I have already said—physical short-comings are so primitive in the main that they keep us below our own average.

It would, for instance, be unnatural to treat both simple nervousness and an inferiority complex at the same time. Naturally, there may be some connection between them, but the complex is due less to nervousness than nervousness is to a complex, so that there are in fact, physical inhibitions which cannot be removed by preparatory exercises alone. Any psychopathological symptom (small or large) can only be removed causally, that is, by attacking the ground on which it flourishes. For this reason, it will often happen that although the symptom may have disappeared during the exercise itself, nothing at all may have changed in everyday life, and the nervous symptom still affects us as unpleasantly as before. Please do not forget that we have not even started with meditation: we have only attacked the basis: the short-comings of our physical bodies and some, but only a few of the internal inhibitions, and that we have only prepared a starting-point for meditation proper.

To those who do not know what true meditation is, these exercises will soon appear very positive and productive, and that is how it should be; but they must not be confused with meditation proper, or what is worse, become a substitute for the real thing.

Before completing this chapter, I should briefly like to compare the conditions of the Asiatic with our own. Are the same inhibitions at work in both cases?

What inhibits us in the first place?—our restlessness, our nerves, our sense of time!

We have spoken above of the ability of the Asiatic to do nothing. The positive results of this "short-coming" are his enviably strong nerves, his unlimited time and his great peacefulness which often passes our understanding, and which to us may become a a great experience.

Imagine the following in a Western capital: Bombay! Five o'clock in the afternoon and rush-hour, as everywhere in the world at that time. By a Bombay police order, only as many passengers may enter a bus or a tram as there are seats in it. Standing passengers are not allowed; yet, as all other Indian cities, Bombay is over-populated; the Indian seems to like "being about". At certain times of the day therefore, queues up to 100 yards long can be seen standing at every stop, waiting for an empty seat to be allocated to them.

Here I had ample opportunity of convincing myself, sometimes for two whole hours, of the fatalistic peace of these Indians. Nobody would think of criticizing these laws which condemn him to endless waiting; let alone jumping the queue.

The same is the case with the doctor or the lawyer:

The consulting- and waiting-room are combined into one, for why should one have secrets? If, during the consulting hours, a good friend of the doctor comes to visit him, then the consultation is interrupted, tea and betel nuts are fetched (generally by the patient himself), and then there is a chat for about an hour. When the friend has gone, the consultation may proceed. Nobody complains.

Now let us imagine this happening here. We just cannot understand such things, and quite naturally so, for we are masters of activity, while the Asiatic has a genius for passivity, the most popular expression of which is found in Gandhi's policy of passive resistance.

Far from wishing to idealize this completely passive patience, we must nevertheless admit that we are on the very opposite side of the scales, and that we fall into the opposite extreme—absolute impatience—much too often.

Be this "over-patience" bad or not, at least it is a token of the inner peace of the average Asiatic, his natural capacity for meditation, and his lack of inner obstacles, all of which bring about immeasurably more favourable conditions than we have.

Surely, it would be desirable to be capable of repose under similar circumstances, for there are moments in life when it could be of the greatest advantage.

How many things have we not borrowed and adopted for our own purposes from the Asiatic over the years: religions, culture, legends, artistic and spiritual elements, all of which are today considered as our very own, down to numerous commercial products.

And we have given no less: Germanic elements of speech are easily recognized even in the modern Asiatic languages; Aryan racial characteristics are found in half of Asia; some elements of Indian Temple architecture show a Nordic influence, yes, in Gāndhāra art Hellenic and Indian ideals are mixed; and even in deepest Turkistan we find temple paintings reminiscent of the frescoes of Mediaeval Gothic churches. And these characteristics can be found as far as Mongolian West Tibet. From these mixed elements the most highly-developed cultures have originated.

Surely, all this should make us a little more interested in meditation, even though it is not a typically Eastern possession.

D

THE PROBLEM OF OUR ENVIRONMENT

WHEN we are asleep our surroundings do not interest us. Although they are there, we do not feel them at all. When we are awake, however, they do play a role, for our inner peace depends on them. What is decisive, however, is not the so-called true nature of the environment, but our picture of it.

Should somebody tell Mr. Miller that "a gentleman from the police is here to see you", he becomes panic-stricken. Is this the fault of the gentleman from the police? No, it is due to Mr. Miller's conscience. Quite unequivocally—for if his conscience were clear, he would not have worried.

Thus, it is only a question of what inner responses are awakened by external concepts and pictures.

Dreams follow an opposite path: out of our conscience and our needs, they create concepts and pictures which, in their turn, will occupy us on the following day, and will thus keep both conscience and needs before our eyes. It is for this reason that a clear conscience is the best pillow.

If we are alone in our room, we feel quite different, and our attention is guided along quite different paths than if somebody else is with us. This is ninety per cent due to the fact *that* somebody is with us and only ten per cent to *who* is with us.

"Man alone" is quite different from "Man in society".

If we visit the sick, we get a certain feeling, we breathe in the smell of the white corridors, their "atmosphere".

If somehow we have dealings with a school, then although we may be ninety years old, the atmosphere will throw us back eighty years.

If we walk across a cemetery, our spirits are automatically damped; if, however, we enter our local pub, they become high just as automatically.

And all this because our momentary locality has become a concept—because the same concept is always expressed in the same external circumstances, and thus produces the corresponding mental and physical reactions. Why have we cited so many strange examples? Because we wish to create a favourable atmosphere for meditation.

Before telling the reader which is the most favourable atmosphere, he should try to answer this question from his own experience. To do so, he must know what precisely is meant by environmental influences. He must proceed strictly analytically because here he can easily be misled.

There is one concept which answers the question about a favourable atmosphere most clearly, and that is *home environment*. If we can answer it, then we have given a picture of our ideal atmosphere. Every man, even the most humble, has his particular conception of his ideal surroundings which is not only the ownership of the things around him, but also the inner impression of well-being, the *knowledge* (and nothing else) of belonging here, both in the inner and the outer self!

It is primarily due to inner attitudes that we choose our clothes, which are not at all—as we are often told—only for other people to look at. "Clothes maketh Man"—not only for others, but for the wearer himself; just as the costume helps an actor to "change" his inner self. Even the negative aspect of this question is of no small significance. The psychological tragedy of our times is not least due to the fact that for one reason or another, few men are in a position to determine their environmental conditions, their "psychogenetic nourishment".

It is the environment which forms the "soul" of the child; it orders the grown-up socially; it creates both the form and the scope of our "struggle for life", and it determines for each one of us—and thus generally—the social aspect of the nation. Especially in the European West where the gap between rich and poor is not so terrifying as in Asia—many "essentials" have become less important in the course of the last thirty, and especially during the last ten years. People who apparently "needed" luxuries, have had to learn greater modesty (often as victims of authority) and to reduce their needs so much that they are satisfied with a mere modicum of what previously appeared to be essential. Satisfied? Yes, even happy. There is a decisive difference between a fraction and an essence—if I have to make do with a mere fraction of what I need, then I suffer; if, however, I know how to obtain the essence, then I lack nothing. Here, too, concentration means the renunciation of that which is not important. Man's very nature leads him to this: he is inclined to neglect those who "mean" less to him, will never leave anything lying about which is "dear to his heart", but will very often forget those things which, although they have a practical value, are not spiritual necessities—such as umbrellas, gloves, brief-cases, etc. This proves that the final decision between what is a "spiritual need" and a "practical necessity" is made by the unconscious and not by reason.

What conclusions can we draw from these facts?

In order not to waste our energy on the unimportant, it is advisable to take stock from time to time—even if only theoretically—of the things which are apparently dear to our hearts, and to imagine what would happen if we were to lose them.

If thus, by means of a conscious clarification of our values, we have gained a certain inner harmony with our own environmental needs, then quietly and deeply convinced of the true orientation of our innermost selves, we can start our preparations for meditation[1].

In what follows we shall chat about the most favourable external conditions for meditation, and the results of our consideration can, for the major part, already be applied to the preparatory exercises described in the previous chapters. This will not necessarily make them easier, but we shall thus become used more quickly to what will become a necessity in a later stage of inner contemplation.

[1] Such convictions are subject to the law of constant change, and cannot be influenced directly, but gain their form and strength from the manner in which we see, judge, accept or reject our environment. Man without environment, let us assume this possibility theoretically, could neither create nor change his inner self, for he would lack an outer measure of his inner relationships. And thus the inner self of Man is not, *a priori*, decisive, but only in his *momentary* relationship to his environment. Only here his latent tendencies can break through, only here can he prove the force of his inner self, and only here can he make decisions, for here he has learned to measure his energy and he has learned where he can vanquish and where he is weak. It is for this reason that it is wrong to desire to by-pass the depths of life, simply in order to live an internally harmonious life. Not the lack of movement in the stream of life creates harmony, but our own proven force against which the crests and troughs of the waves break without effect. Meditation is to help us to create this force, not, however, to shield us from the arrows of life behind an umbrella of ecstatic half-living. Not the ostrich is the symbol of the Buddha, but the elephant; and in the Indian coat of arms there is neither the hare nor the owl, but the Lion.

To him who is not yet a master, meditation will not be possible at any time and in any environment. Just as the beginner in music may not immediately perform the great classics, but must first prepare the ground for them by easier exercises, so the beginner in meditation must take stock of his own short-comings and must make do with the necessary requirements determined by his own capacities; this he will do the more readily the more he knows that it is only in systematic progress that he can hope for success.

THE ROOM

AFTER what we have just said, it must be clear that the room itself is of almost decisive importance for meditation.

Be as careful as possible in its choice, for this room is to be dedicated to our purpose exclusively for as long as is humanly possible.

"Dedicated", I say, and I mean it literally, for meditation must never be considered a hobby, but rather as something as important as going to church, or to a festive ceremony. If this seems an exaggerated demand, please tell me of any other reason for going to church than the salvation of your own soul. And this is just what we do in meditation.

"Man, look within yourself!" is the slogan in both cases.

The best thing we can do to further meditation is to have a room—a little one will suffice—for this purpose alone. To most of you this may sound like ridiculous theory, for you may not even possess a study of your own.

Strange as it may sound, if the choice were yours a room for meditation is more desirable than a study; for if meditation is successful, it is not difficult to concentrate on work, even during the hustle and bustle of family life; but if you can find no inner peace, work will hardly progress even behind sound-proof doors. Yet only a few will have at their disposal a whole room, however small, for the exclusive purpose of a daily half-hour of meditation. We must and we shall take this fact into consideration. However, in many Asiatic countries such a room *is* part of every house, and just as much taken for granted as a bath-room or a dining-room is in the West.

If the worst comes to the worst we can do the following:

If we have a study, or any other room at all which is not regularly used by the family, a small corner of it might be divided off for our purpose by means of a screen, a curtain, or a partition. It is important to create a symbolical island of absolute peace and reflection—one not desecrated by nervousness and excitement. This may appear as an empty phrase, a

54

mere phantasy: but just take the case of our own bed. Do you remember the time when you were at the other end of town, when you had missed your last bus and it was raining, and you desired nothing so much as your own bed? Why not your easy chair or the dining-table? Why did you have to long just for your bed? Because for you and for us all it is the very essence of relaxation—because every time you lie on it you think, "The whole world can go hang!"

It is just the same here! During the day, too, we need a place where the whole world can go hang as far as we are concerned—into which we can escape when we are worried beyond description, and where innermost peace awaits us like a loving mother.

Certainly, it takes quite some time for our little sanctum to gain this power; but you may be certain that the time will come, and that it will be well worth while.

Please be careful not to take any cares into it. In the beginning this is discouragingly difficult; but we shall return to this question later on. Here, we only wish to deal with the material preparations.

Let us assume that a small room is at our disposal, and let us now adapt it to our purposes. This would be simple if all requirements were at hand. Simple, yes, but it can't be done. Nothing here must affect our soul which has become an everyday concept; nothing which could recall any previous use. Unless the objects had been holy even before—such as a prayer book, a hymn book, a crucifix or similar object.

No chair, no table. What good would they do? We shall sit on the floor. Of course, we shall need something to make squatting on the floor more comfortable; but of this later.

We need only one thing, and although many of you will not agree with me, I do know why I say it—a small Buddha. Why?

For quite some time to come we shall be bothered by external thoughts and cares, and it might happen only too easily that they so overwhelm us, that we start brooding and forget the real purpose of our being there. We need a monitor who shows us the way to better thinking, and whose deep inner peace becomes our guiding star.

Meditation is a part of all religions; but no one has realized this more than Gotama Buddha. He considered meditation for the sake of transcendental results as useless, for as he said: "What good is it to know the Universe if I cannot make peace with my inner self? What good is it to look for Gods if I do not even know what takes place in my soul?" It is he who taught mankind the way to the sources of consciousness, taught it to recognize *what* is responsible for sorrow and suffering, taught it to ask consistently for the causes and not to blame "Fate" for man's own inadequacies.

"You can do it," he said; "therefore do it! I have shown you the way, for I have followed it myself. You are not the victims of an external law, but of internal causes."

Humanity has come to appreciate the essence of his wisdom during the two and a half thousand years of the existence of his teaching, which has given man its simplest and most symbolic expression in the image of the great teacher himself. This image does not claim to be a monument to his own person, but makes the far greater claim that it is the symbolical expression of his wisdom, and of his great peacefulness—which, in his own life and by realizing his own doctrine in himself, he made a practical reality. Never and nowhere is the image meant to be an icon.

Those who are deeply rooted in their own religion, and would not even think of becoming converts to Buddhism, need never fear that they would be accepting "another religion" and thus committing a sin against their own, for nobody expects them to pray to the Buddha. Indeed, to do so would not only outrage their own convictions, but would run counter to the teachings of the Buddha himself.

Our Buddha image is meant only to irradiate us with the wise reflection of many centuries which have gone into the form of his image: spiritual peace, sublimity, inner integrity, the material embodiment of meditation.

It is not important that we become converted to his teachings, and by adopting his intellectual principles merely create a twilight state between inexperienced religion and semi-spiritual philosophy. In any case, we must avoid making the most common blunder of the West, which consists of dissecting everything down to the finest detail intellectually, and then to consider the human being simply as a well-functioning machine with nothing behind the works, whose glandular functions represent the last word in knowledge. We do not want to consider our Buddha image as an image, but as a symbol of what we wish to become; this changes nothing in our religion, just as it changes nothing in our family life.

Yet, even if one day it should change anything in our religion, then it is certainly not the fault of the image; it is due to quite different causes.

I need not stress that I am not addressing Buddhists here, but I can see no reason why all books about meditation have to start from the standpoint of the Buddhist; as if millions of Christians did not have the same need for inner peace. The Buddha has never said: "I have created a new religion," and in principle has done no more than to show mankind the best path to the sources of its own freedom; never did he forbid non-believers to follow this path. Never has he made the practice of his teaching dependent on religious beliefs.

We shall place this small Buddha a little above us, so that while we are seated, the entire figure can enter our field of vision whenever necessary.

A few quiet, beautiful pictures: perhaps a landscape by Turner, an etching by Dürer or Rethel, a painting of a flower by Meer—this is all our small sanctuary will contain . . .

Apart from a. vase! For whenever possible, we shall have fresh flowers in our room.

I need hardly stress that the room must always be spotlessly clean. In a clean room it is much easier to have clean thoughts. This cleaning must be done by *ourselves*. Every day!

Mr. Miller shakes his head:

"And in this empty room you expect me to feel at home? If there isn't even a shred of comfort, I shall be afraid every time I have to enter it."

We have nothing against comfort; but would Fate itself listen to this objection before cruelly forcing us to do without it?

It is just for this reason that we want the very minimum of those things which we may lose at any moment. It is just because we want to learn how to be at home in our innermost selves rather than amongst the furniture of our house. We want to learn what it means "to be at home", without clutching at the easy chair, the library, the radio, the newspaper or the coffee-table.

These things will never lose their significance in our everyday life just because we gain a much deeper understanding of the meaning of "home"; rather shall we learn to estimate their true value far more correctly. It is less dangerous to rejoice in possessions and yet to renounce them with a smile when necessary. To own something must not mean to be irretrievably lost in it.

Once upon a time there lived in Peking a great connoisseur and collector—the wise Wu. One day the merchant Wei came to visit him, for they were childhood friends. And the wise Wu showed his collection to the merchant Wei.

"This," he said, pointing to a colourful dragon, the size of a crocodile, made of the finest porcelain, "this is is my proudest possession! Look! It is the finest and rarest of porcelains ever to have been fired in the Middle Empire; and I will confide to you that in the whole world there are only two of these extremely valuable dragons: this one here, and the Emperor's. Each of them—please do be seated my friend— is worth one hundred and fifty thousand yen."

The merchant Wei, who had never heard of so vast a sum of money—for he was a modest merchant—got such a fright that he collapsed, and unfortunately in falling, he broke the valuable dragon, which splintered into 150,000 fragments.

"From this moment on," said the wise Wu, smiling painfully, "the dragon of the Emperor will be worth three hundred thousand yen."

In our meditation room we shall be at a distance from things and the world, and this distance we shall shape into a living space, for as soon as our own intellect begins to become crystal clear, we shall recognize that the things of our environment, however helpful, are never part of ourselves.

I say: we recognize it. We do not need to try to *convince* ourselves of it, for this is one of the most basic results of meditation: Truth is recognized by itself alone, and to find it nothing is needed but a receptive heart. Who, however, would believe that truth could flow into an unclean vessel?

OUR CLOTHES

THE title of this chapter sounds pedantic. But it is not pedantic to discuss this point also, it is just being careful. Please believe me.

In every important undertaking we always think of our clothes; the more important the occasion, the more careful we are.

For church, for a festival, for the theatre, for a ball, for a birthday celebration, even for the dance floor, we dress more elegantly, i.e. more carefully than we do for our humdrum everyday lives. And this has become so natural to us that we hardly think about it any more. Who could expect to be gay if he went to a ball in his working clothes? Every dress creates its own special atmosphere, more so for ourselves than for others. And if at night we usually change our coat in order to be more comfortable, then it is less for *direct* physical comfort (for, after all, our coat wasn't all that uncomfortable), than for psychological comfort, which gives rise to immediate physical satisfaction.

We are used to putting most of everyday life out of our minds when our daily work is done, and if only by changing coats or shoes, or by washing, we try to become somebody else.

Shouldn't we also try to become "somebody else" by means of meditation? Shouldn't we try to put as much as possible out of mind?

With every part of our everyday self that we take with us, we also carry part of its cares. The very pockets of our working clothes are lined with these cares, and at the slightest opportunity they creep out. This is particularly harmful to meditation.

What then should we do? The answer is simple: we must change our clothes.

For this we need not take out our Sunday suit. We need nothing more than "a change", something absolutely *clean* which in future will be worn only in the meditation room and nowhere else at all. It·will hang on a nail on the door of the room (inside!).

Meditation begins the very moment that we put on these clothes, just as a gay mood becomes even gayer the very moment that we put on our best suit.

What we wear makes very little difference. It can be ugly and it can be simple. Only it must have nothing which reminds us of previous use. Further, it must be clean and immaculate, and must be washed and ironed more frequently than is absolutely necessary.

I admit that all this sounds like a strange rite; and it would be just that, if we were not aware that it is only a psychological measure, which can be explained at great length. It is just in this light, and only in this light, that the Japanese sees it, and he takes great pains over this "dress ritual".

The shoes are also taken off (before entering the room if possible); for they would not only impair squatting and be uncomfortable in many respects, but what applies to the suit applies to them even more forcibly: the outer world sticks to them.

Let us sum up: everything which reminds us of "outside" stays outside, and everything which is not spotlessly clean must either be changed or cleaned.

Here Mr. Miller will pipe up again:

"There's something that I fail to understand. You said that meditation would give me a clearer vision of my soul, my sorrows and my life. Very well. But how can you reconcile all this with your blatant efforts to create the greatest possible distance from everyday life, from cares, and the world outside?

"It is my purpose to create an inviolable island. That may be very well for a half-hour; but how can I ameliorate my careworn everyday life while sitting on this island? How from this entirely new world, isolated as I am and with eyes closed and thoughts controlled, can I hope to master my problems? Is this just another form of self-deception?"

It is a known fact that things assume an entirely different aspect from a distance. When rage has evaporated and passion has abated, everything looks quite different; and we are often near despair at the thought that again we have lost self-control and have acted like fools.

It is then that we look at our actions objectively as if at another's, and somehow we have in fact, become "another". Yet, we do not know if tomorrow we shall not *again* be the same, making the same or even new mistakes. We do not know it, for although we think that we know ourselves so "well", we cannot rely upon ourselves at all. In small things perhaps; but in questions of passion. . . .

Therefore let us gain distance. This will raise our inner life above the confused kaleidoscope of the world around us— will rob it of any possible excuses, such as important work, family duties, inclinations or necessities; will put it on the dissection table, naked so that it can be investigated.

Yet it will be as obstinate as possible. Haven't we all experienced that although we knew how to act, think and feel differently, nevertheless for one reason or another, we acted wrongly because we gave in to some weakness. Do we want to assume the 'weaknesses" as given facts?

Obviously we must do so as long as we consider them merely as "weaknesses", without recognizing their hidden sources; but when we have removed all possibilities of self-deception (white and not-so-white lies), then we shall be forced into the open.

It is grotesque that these weaknesses do not even baulk at using the most simple things in the world around us, such as our dress, as veiled excuses.

The old masters knew all this instinctively and showed humanity naked and bare before the final judgment.

Let us therefore, free ourselves from the spell of these so-called necessities before we appoint ourselves judges of our behaviour. Let us make things easier for ourselves (for it is nothing else) by not erecting those walls in the first place which may later become a hindrance. If in what follows we refer to a number of apparently ridiculous, unimportant, pedantic or naïve requirements, the reader is asked to suspend judgment for a little while, for it is only too possible that a derisive smirk may close those portals behind which reverent astonishment awaits him.

THE RIGHT POSTURE FOR MEDITATION

THE well-known oriental way of squatting crosslegged deserves a whole chapter. It is a constant source of dispute amongst those skilled in the ways of meditation, for they cannot agree whether this form of squatting is decisive for the success of meditation.

The representatives of each of their opinions believe that they have reason on their side, and the reader may decide for himself whether he will side with the theoreticians who consider it irrelevant, or with the practitioners who attach great importance to it.[1]

Up to now we have refused to consider unfounded theories and in this instance, too, we shall stick to our principles. Let us, therefore, admit at once that the "Lotus Posture" is not strictly necessary in theory, yet that it is of great significance for any practical success. We shall explain its necessity here so that it can then be learned without great effort.

There are many reasons for, and only one reason against, this form of squatting. Only at first is it a little uncomfortable, but as soon as this difficulty is overcome, the reasons for it become clearer.

In the first place, sitting on a chair compared with sitting on the floor, is extremely mechanical and unnatural.

Let us imagine that we have wandered into the open, that we have climbed up the mountain and that we are now enjoying the distant beauty as in a dream—the silence of the heavens and of the landscape, the perfume of the grass, the breathing earth—let us imagine that we do all this sitting on a chair.

That's a queer thought, isn't it?

We are accustomed to seeing the Buddha in the Lotus posture, and it is in this way that the layman invariably imagines him. It is interesting, however, to find stone images

---

[1] This typically Asiatic form of squatting is—especially in its religious applications—not at all so "typically Asiatic". The meditative posture of Christian mystics is very similar to it, especially in the form (see below) explained here.

See F. Heiler *Bodily Posture in Prayer*, Hommel-Festchrift (Mitt. d. vorderas. Ges. 1916).

of a preaching Buddha in a "Western posture" in the Pandu-
lena Caves near Nasik, and we immediately get the feeling
that something is wrong here. These images do not radiate
absolute peace in the same way as the familiar Buddha does.
Something seems to speak to us, something seems to be *at
work* (and this is as it should be), while the Lotus posture
automatically creates the impression of inner harmony, of
absorption rather than of "work".

Even today this difference is kept alive in India; I, the
teacher, always had to sit a little higher, while my native
pupils would squat Lotus-fashion on the floor. I was "active",
while they were "absorptive".

In any event, we wish to achieve a compact posture. It is
important that the extremities should be as near the body as
possible. This can obviously be done by pulling the knees
up into a squatting position; unfortunately the body becomes
squashed and the blood circulation is unnecessarily impeded.
Apart from this, we tend to fall over backwards. The fear of
this happening naturally means the end of every attempt to
meditate.

Why should our arms and legs be as close to the body as
possible? In order to put them under the immediate control
of consciousness. The fact that consciousness is less effective in
stretched-out extremities is easily demonstrated.

It is, for instance, a well-known fact that for one reason
or another, we tap on the table if we are nervous. If, however,
the hand should happen to be close to us, we only start tapping
on the table when our excitement and irritation have become
extreme—i.e. when controlling consciousness is almost completely overcome by the source of excitation. Conversely, when
our arms are far away from the body, this tapping is meaningless and insignificant, and is not even noticed.

Meditation, however, is particularly concerned with
bringing those things to our conscious attention which are
normally not noticed, and to test their value.

The above equally applies to the feet. Twitching toes
belong to the same family as tapping fingers: pathologically
meaningless, psychologically significant. If we are just *slightly*
nervous and want to become less so simply by giving our hands
and feet free rein, we should realize that this does not *"work*

off" anything, but is a mere *manifestation*. If we had a clock to measure nervousness, we should come to the surprising conclusion that finger-tapping, etc., unmistakably *increases* nervousness, and that there can be no question of any "working off" at all.

Thus, the nearer the hands and feet are to the body, the more attentively they are watched by our subconscious. This is precisely what happens in the Lotus posture.

The faithful promise: "I can watch my hands and feet even without bothering with the Lotus posture!" is encouraging, but nevertheless unacceptable, for after all we do not meditate to watch over our limbs. We have much more important work to do.

It may sound odd, but have you ever considered that your feet feel "stranger" to you than your hands only because your feet are "farther away"? Farther away from what? From watching consciousness!

It is for this reason that they lead a much more independent life than our hands which, too, at times, are apt to play of their own accord with a handkerchief, a bunch of keys, a match-box or a cigarette-case. But their "own accord" is by no means as great as that of our feet, even though the feet have a much more limited sphere of action.

We know just how we move our hands even if we don't watch them; but we become aware of the movements of our feet only when we pay careful attention to them—which happens only in the rarest of cases.

There are some extremely clever practical psychologists who control their fellow-men not by studying their faces, but by watching the hands and the feet of their "victims", because these have a life of their own which most clearly betrays what goes on underneath. The power of controlling consciousness reaches them only so weakly, or only if they are deliberately watched, that they betray much more than facial expression. All this should make it clear that here, too, concentration and control are important, though not for the purpose of deceiving our fellow-men.

Since we do not yet possess an "anatomy of the soul" which would enable us to delimit the effective realm of controlling consciousness—as we can delimit blood circulation or respiration—we must rely on the experience of those people who have such an anatomy, i.e. the Indians of ancient times.

Let us imagine a vertebral column as a yard-stick, its lowest pole a minus and its highest—the top of the skull—a plus.[1] Controlling consciousness is effective between both these poles. Naturally it also extends to the tips of our toes and fingers—we need not stress this—but there it has lost much of its intensity.

A child who is afraid of having his hand injured, instinctively pulls his arms towards his body to bring them under the protection of his controlling consciousness. Conversely, those who (for instance when visiting a doctor) do not wish to minimize pain in their hands, but rather want to feel it more strongly, will push their hands as far away from the body as possible.

In this connection it is interesting to note that the pain is not physiologically *lessened* thereby, but that an attempt is made to ignore it psychologically. Neuro-physiological perception depends on the amount of blood circulating through the organ in question.[2]

Man assumes that he cannot regulate pain by *himself* (he could learn this without any great effort), and so he attempts to remove it from immediate perception. "Don't think of it and then it won't hurt!" is a common way of speaking.

As we have stressed time after time, in meditation there is no conscious ignoring of any part of our personality. On the contrary, we try to do everything possible to produce a harmonious relationship between all parts of ourselves. As soon as we have overcome the first obstacles and have established

[1] For further information on the anatomy of Yoga see my book *Der Yogi und der Komödiant* (The Yogi and the Comedian).

[2] Thus, those who, by means of Hatha-Yoga and Pranayama-practice, can consciously affect their blood circulation, may become completely free of pain. Time after time this can be seen when we watch Dervishes, Fakirs, or Yogis, those much maligned men who very often inflict the most horrible wounds upon themselves with needles or daggers, but who apparently feel no pain and do not bleed. Bloodlessness and painlessness therefore go hand in hand.

If severe wounds so inflicted heal uncommonly quickly, sometimes within the space of hours, then this is due to an opposite cause—an extraordinary increase in the blood circulation.

Here we find that the Yogi has a pulse of 130 to 150 beats per minute, and a correspondingly increased temperature.

This can only be achieved through absolute concentration and a special form of breathing. In our meditative exercises, too, we shall become familiar with physiological manifestations which are—at least in their inner character—related to these events.

E

inner and outer peace, we shall discover that it is precisely in the Lotus posture, rather than in what we would still consider a more comfortable one, that the *whole* body, including the extremities, forms a strangely compact unit. There is no need to try to establish this, to talk ourselves into it—we shall very soon be able to notice it.

This posture, as soon as it is mastered, will be found extremely comfortable and of further advantage. Let us save ourselves the trouble of a long investigation into the reasons and simply accept the strange fact that sitting in our habitual manner increases *intellectual* thinking; the Lotus posture, however, favours *intuitive* thinking. Genius is always closer to the earth than the intellect—even physically.

How do we apply this knowledge to our greatest practical advantage?

We could only sit like Orientals, who are used to crossing both legs and arms from earliest childhood, after years of patient and sometimes painful training. Even so, most of us could only learn it so imperfectly that it would not be an advantage at all.

For this reason we simply attempt to approach as near to the "original" as possible, and do not waste too much time, effort and energy on it.

Let us start from the well-known position of squatting cross-legged. This has a number of disadvantages:

1. One leg presses upon the other.
2. Our back has no support and for this reason we are apt to lean on our arms or knees, or to bend forward so much that we become unnecessarily and unsuitably contorted.
3. It is not relaxing, and relaxation is the alpha and omega of all meditation.
4. The body is squashed.
5. We can see no advantage in sitting on the floor and feel uncomfortable.

Nevertheless, this position is the starting-point which we shall adapt for purposes of comfort and suitability:

To begin with, we shall take a thick cushion and fold it

into a roll of a hand's breadth; and on this roll (laid crosswise) we shall sit. What could not be done before—putting our legs flat on the floor and crossing them—can now be managed with ease, since the weight of the body has now been shifted to the front.

This is how things look now:

One leg is so flat on the floor that the heel of the foot can support the body, as the heel lies close to the "crutch" (directly below the genital region). The other leg is also flat, either close in front of the first with the soles almost touching it, or bent even more with the foot resting near the instep or the peroneal muscle. If the cushion is too high, the heel will press too strongly; if it is too low the upper thigh will feel slightly strained.

By now it will have become crystal clear that this posture is as comfortable as any, even if—let us admit it—only for a limited period of time at the start. It must become a habit first. The hands rest, palms upwards, one upon the other in the lap. The upper part of the body is neither bent forward nor does the chest stand out. The head has a slight tendency towards the front, and we may say that the most comfortable and the most suitable position of the head is when the nose makes an angle of 45 degrees with the floor.

Sitting thus, the question of whether or not we may support ourselves does not even arise, for when the weight is evenly distributed, there is no need for support at all. Instead, we have a slight tendency to bend forward, and that does not matter much, for bending forward means inclining towards attention, bending backwards, however, produces a tendency to sleep.

The upper part of the body is freer than when we squat cross-legged, even freer than sitting on a chair, where we either fall to the front or, more frequently, into a sleeping tendency of lazy support. We can breathe freely and we can relax adequately and much better than sitting on a chair. This we shall find to our great satisfaction, as soon as we have acquired the habit.

We can feel the security of the floor, feel that from this position we cannot fall, that we form a compact field of energy whose centre is where our ancestors placed the seat of the soul, and whence all respiration obtains its driving impulse: the solar plexus.

THE SIXTH SENSE

No man can be blamed for not knowing, but only misjudging what he does know.

We often consider things as unimportant although they are not, and conversely we often waste time and energy on what is utterly insignificant. This is a fault inherent in "erring humanity"; not even Goethe was beyond reproach, for he believed that his scientific investigations would make him eternally famous.

We have no sense organ for the absolute; and since we can only judge by results, anything that has no direct manifestations, that can only be grasped intuitively, or on the basis of inferences and generalized laws, must remain inaccessible to experience.

We cannot perceive "motion" directly, but only as "change of place" with time. "Time" cannot be perceived either, only "processes" of change, by which we artificially measure time as the duration of the processes. "Space" is imperceptible— we are only aware of the relationship of two points to each other, and the time which is needed to relate one point to the next. This creates a concept of time, but by no means an absolute one. Sense organs therefore, are nothing but coarse aids to consciousness, which in its turn is handicapped by being tied to pictures and concepts.

People who consider that only their sense perceptions matter, always ask for proof, yet they could easily discover that a proof by the senses is less valid than a mathematical one, and that an intuitive proof can refute even the mathematical.

It is true that contemporary science does not go far enough, even if it went a long way when Einstein proved that the mathematics of the Cosmos, i.e. true mathematics, is not logical. Thus, the shortest way is not the "straight line"— "straight lines" do not even exist—parallel lines can become intertwined and good old Euclid was quite wrong.

As long as we are not ever ready to sacrifice any given datum of rational science to an intuitive idea, science will always keep silent about absolute truth, or even about absolute knowledge which alone can explain the mechanics of our universe satisfactorily. Even the most exact science has always involved illogical magnitudes, such as zero and infinity.

Thus, although all the suggestions made in this book are based on experience, only a part can be proved by rational science, and yet the rest is no metaphysical speculation, since it, too, has been proved empirically.

So-called modern science, that is the science of the last hundred years, refuses to recognize intuitive experience as valid, since it does not completely correspond with analytical experience. It has not yet discovered any connection between intellect and intuition, and is hopelessly lost outside the atrophied system of logico-intellectual analysis. This is under-standable from the point of view of intellectual synthesis, but not from that of those who wish to obtain practical results from intuitive experience, and who do not place any value on a positivistic, i.e. intellectual system of classification. They prefer to "work" with the organless sixth sense called either the "soul", or by any other scientifically unfounded name.

Science is quite right when it refuses to recognize the objective existence of the soul. There "is" no soul, for then as logic would have it, it would equally be possible that the soul "is not". Nevertheless, everything seems to point to a "sphere of the soul". Thus we shall just have to accept that there "*is*" something which "is not". (By the way, the same applies to character also.)

For this reason the mediaeval tripartition of man into body, spirit and soul is by no means "naïve and outworn", it is only—and this is a gigantic process—shorn of its material character and thus raised to an infinitely higher level.

Nevertheless, it would be dangerous to ask: If the mediaeval concept of spirit and soul was wrong, what is the *right* concept according to our greater knowledge?

Every concept of spirit and soul is false as long as it is merely a "concept", i.e. a "picture".

Let us put it quite unscientifically: there are things which we must take into account without being able to prove them objectively. This is known by everybody who can feel; but those who are cursed by having to think about everything, will always land up in the Middle Ages with all its undeveloped ideas of the soul and of intuition. Woe to him who believes that the spirit is no more than thought! Our idea of the world is not formed by our thought, but by the importance which we attach to this thought. If we were to take the results of thought as absolute then the world, too, would be absolute. If, on the other hand, we recognize the limits of our thought, then we automatically recognize the limits of our environment. From this it follows that the world around us merely forms the basis of our consciousness (without which there would be no world at all), and that our intuition, in so far as it does not involve thought, and realizing the limits of mentation, has a far greater sphere of action.

Scientifically this cannot be proved as yet, just as only the psychological evolution, not the absolute origin, of concepts such as God, Love, Wisdom, etc., can be explained.

Psychology as a science had for long been working with similar concepts, by constantly assuming an unknown magnitude which, while it can be proved functionally, can never be proven in a concrete scientific manner.

Thus psychology has become a significant and highly-developed subject which—with all its extensions—remains a scientific island. It is true that we can find some path to philosophy from it, but no "bridge" to concrete science. This bridge is called the "soul". To look for it would be just as false as to deny it—to deny the validity of this concept would be just as short-sighted as trying to prove it analytically.

Theoretically much of this remains unsatisfactory, but it is much less so in practice; for we love and hate, have sympathy and antipathy, have no desire for this and are more inclined to that, are happy when the sun is shining, oppressed when it rains, have a weakness for this and no time for that, love little children and little dogs, and always talk about the fact that we are in full control of ourselves and know why and wherefore.

Why is this so? Because it is not intellectual knowledge, but intuition which moulds our "inner attitudes".

Two forms of thought, intuitive and analytical, keep us

constantly on the move, and the one influences the other. At the moment all we need know is that we shall have to consider them both, and that each has its own important task, i.e. each must be treated differently, for each one springs from a different layer of the "soul"; and although they are twin brothers, equally dear to, and equally valued by, the father— the spirit, they have quite opposite characters.

I say opposite, for how else could it come about that now and then we fail to understand ourselves? We know that we ought to do one thing and yet we do the other, that we should have acted thus and that in fact, we did the opposite. Goethe speaks of "two souls" in the breast of Faust.

The one knows that meditation is a good thing; the other objects to the small inconveniences which it entails.

We do not want to meditate for the sake of scientific results, but simply for abstract intuitive ones. We want to get to the roots of instinct in order to cultivate them, so that our harvest of the fruits of the Tree of Life may become richer. Once we realize that certain truths can only be understood intuitively and that our intuition is near the miraculous, then we have already taken the first step towards developing it.

Those who cannot judge intuition in its deepest origins call it prejudice, sentiment, bias, inclination, etc., and as "modern", "clear thinking" men they are inclined to suppress these things as being "unreasonable".

True, intuition has not sprung from calculating reason; but it remains to be seen if the results of this "unreason" do not produce the most natural and the best results. For, in calculated thinking, reason falls asleep; with intuitive thinking, the "unreason" of truth awakes.

On the broad temple steps leading down to the Ganges, there sat a sage. A youth came up to him and said:

"I desire to be your pupil."

"What is your sole and highest aim?" the sage asked.

The eyes of the pupil glowed: "God alone," he said, "is my one and only desire! It is the thought of God alone which fills my entire being."

The sage got hold of the youth by the hair and dipped his head into the waters of the Ganges. The youth almost drowned.

But the wisdom of the sage was great and at the very last moment, he pulled the youth out of the water.

"Now tell me," the sage asked, "what you were longing for most just then?"

"For air," the truth-loving youth replied.

"I see," said the sage; "and what of your thoughts of God?"

The youth smiled: "Pray, Master, in such a situation air is more important even than God!"

How unreasonable—how human!

THE CHOICE OF TIME

THERE is hardly anybody who has unlimited leisure. We are usually free at certain hours of the day, and the hours during which we are occupied are usually just as definitely fixed. Thus, the time for meditation is determined from the start. We do not need a whole chapter to arrive at so obvious a conclusion. However, we do wish to consider what influence the time of day has on us and on meditation.

Let us preface our remarks by stating that it is essential to stick to the chosen time, and that while we may change it a little on occasion, and even sometimes miss it if absolutely necessary, we may never change it "just to suit ourselves".

The best hours for meditation are at dawn and at dusk, and of the two, dawn is preferable. Since in winter the day usually begins before sunrise, it is possible to regulate meditation not by the clock, but by the sun; by changing the time a little each day we ensure that meditation always ends just as the sun rises.

The worst time is noon; late mornings and afternoons are also of little use, while the night is extremely favourable.

I wonder if it is not more than an accident that the power for meditation almost exactly corresponds to the sensitivity of a radio-receiver. For here, too, there is a so-called twilight effect.

The sun is not only the symbol of activity, it radiates activity; and the "mood" which it transmits to us in its summery rays is not only one of great joy—but also puts us into immediate contact with the life force which quickens not only man and beasts but plants as well. This is good, and as it should be; but activity is something creative, while meditation is not creative but expectant; not dynamic but static—a deliberate moving out of the circle of time in order to obey the natural law of tension and relaxation.

We can see this law of Nature in the waking of the day and the sleep of night; but only to the most primitive is waking no more than the opposite of sleep. To the more sensitive, consciousness is a state of tension and of constant creation, whose opposite he seeks and finds in the relaxation of expectant silence, in the great inner peace of meditation.

Thus, the primitive person is in greater need of religious ritual than the more sensitive one who attaches greater importance to the *meaning* of the ritual. The *plane* on which tension and relaxation takes place is decisive; and while to the primitive all creation ends in material manifestations and all resting is merely a "creative pause", to the more developed person tension and relaxation are merely the twin processes of spiritual respiration, creation and self-collection in the continuous life stream; he experiences a liberation from the shackles of matter, from the shackles of time. The flow will then change direction and proceed from within the core of experience to the work outside; and absorption of experience will, in its turn, nourish this core so that it can emerge refreshed.

This can be seen on the larger scale in our work and in our wrestling with its problems, and on the smaller scale in the course of the day.

What we create in daylight we must account for at night; what we create in the bright and vibrant world, is judged by the silent, dark judge of nightly self-recollection.

What happens at night looks quite different in the light of day. Slighter, less important and less relevant. True, it may be more optimistic, but isn't "optimism" often an excuse for "irrelevance"?

Optimism is one of the greatest treasures of humanity; but it becomes a scourge if we use it to lie facts out of the way, instead of paying attention. We alone are the victims of our faults.

Therefore, we must carefully choose the time of "judgment", of creative breathing, of avowal, the hours of silence. Here we become free of external shackles only the more to fill the active hours which are to follow with our newly won experience. Meditation is no mere manipulation—for *we, ourselves* are its result.

In meditation we do not decide, we simply change. Just as the clouds do not change the sun but only veil it, so the absolute in us is only hidden by the fog of deception.

Early-morning meditation, *after* washing (for we must be spotlessly clean) and *before* breakfast (for a full stomach is an obstacle) is the most beneficial.

Since in the first year we shall not exceed half an hour, we shall not have to sacrifice too much sleep, nor any part of the working-day.

The fact that morning is the best time is proved by the many benefits which ensue during the rest of the day. It is obvious that a day ended with a stocktaking of ourselves is equally beneficial.

In the beginning we shall not attain a very deep understanding of our true selves—this can only develop with time. Our meditating twice a day will not make us more *successful* in our deeper understanding. However, we need not bother so much with future achievements as with fulfilling the demands of the day. For this, a quarter or a half an hour extra can only be to the good.

Those who can, should choose the early morning. They will be rewarded much sooner than they expect.

SOME AFTERTHOUGHTS ON THE PREPARATIONS

WE have now happily passed the stage of preparations. We enumerated them and tried to justify them, we were often long-winded yet never exhaustive. Let us discard prejudice and simply realize that it is the small details which go to make up the whole picture. Far be it from me to wish to dictate how you must follow the path to your own inner strength. You are fully entitled to ignore everything that is said here, and instead proceed along entirely different paths. For after all, why shouldn't you arrive at the goal by another route? Sometime, somehow we always arrive at the goal if only we long for it honestly. It is merely a question of effort, of the length of the path and of the things we must shed on the way.

It isn't even certain that the path outlined (but not invented) by me is the shortest; yet it has proved its worth to many, and it is for this reason that I feel justified in handing it on.

If we wish to take stock of all that has been said so far, then apparently nothing more emerges than a man, who at the break of day squats on the floor of a bare room. But, on drawing an intermediate balance sheet, we shall find that the external is unimportant, insignificant, and may even lead the "unbiased observer" to false conclusions. What is important is the cause within, the inner course of events, and inner results.

The unbiased observer, just because he is intelligent, may arrive all the more quickly at false conclusions, and thus get a wrong impression of our motives. For this reason we shall not bother him with our odd ideas at all, but rather convince *ourselves* that what we do is extremely important.

Meditation is a completely personal matter whose success largely depends on how highly personal we make it. Yes, even if our partner in marriage should wish to follow the same path, we should nevertheless, neither discuss meditation nor its successes.

We may only discuss the difficulties; but even this can become dangerous, for with every intellectual discussion we change our inner orientation. The next exercise will then be governed by quite different and predominantly intellectual, inner motives, destroying much of the inner peace which we have attained.

This is one of the many reasons why a practitioner of meditation only writes books or even holds lectures on the subject with the utmost reluctance. He knows that he is robbing himself, and the Buddha went so far as to forbid his pupils to do so at the threat of expulsion from the order.

It is always best not to occupy oneself intellectually with meditation—its problems and difficulties. Just as we keep the external world out of our thoughts during meditation, so meditation should be kept out during the rest of the day.

Our life should be as pure and open as possible; not for the sake of meditation, for the latter as such is unimportant—but for the sake of our inner life. If, however, we should find a better way to our true inner selves than meditation, then by all means let us follow it. Nevertheless, as long as meditation seems the best way—and after all it has proved itself in religions for many millennia—we can hardly do better than those sages before us: to follow one of the many paths of meditation as the way to higher development and to the liberation of inner forces. For the ways to meditation are as manifold as are the faces around us.

Now we come to meditation proper. If previously we had reason to complain of a lack of concrete indications—we shall have even more reason to do so now, for here everything can only be understood with that sixth sense which we discussed above, and which, thank God, we all have in us, even if science does not recognize it.

Some common sense will help us on this path, unfortunately so abstract. However, on the whole, we shall be working with such concepts as: inner voice, conscience, mood, feelings, rather than with more "reasonable" ones such as nervous system, pain, respiration, etc. We shall be stupid enough not to try to explain the inexplicable, but to see immediate reality in the light of the absolute which is beyond reason. Not because we love the mysterious, but just because our life is a stream and in every stream it is the source which is most important. Our source, however, lies where mere reason cannot reach.

Wouldn't it be interesting to follow the stream as far back as possible? This we shall do, and on its bed we shall discover many precious stones.

MENTAL, SPIRITUAL, AND PHYSICAL ASSUMPTIONS FOR BEGINNING

So far we have merely indicated the internal and[i] external framework, and if the reader should now sit down full of expectations, he will be sorely disappointed. Notwithstanding the great splash that we have made we have achieved nothing so far. It is as if we had accidentally come into possession of a mighty magic formula, and must conclude to our sorrow that we can achieve nothing with it.

The main part begins only now, just as magic formulae are not effective in themselves, but depend on the magician. There is nothing magical about meditation, and those who have taken this analogy literally only show that they have not understood a single thing in this book.

If now, by setting aside regular periods of time to "lying still", we have rid ourselves of those physical complaints which hamper meditation and which generally occupy most of our energy, and divert it from the actual aim, we have passed the stage of preparations.

We have achieved some small measure of "peace" which, although it is a considerable achievement, is nevertheless only the beginning.

Indeed, even what we shall achieve considerably later, the cessation of bodily sensation, is also no more than a beginning. Nevertheless it must neither be over- nor under-estimated. While it is no anaesthetic, no means of becoming completely free of sensation, it is yet essential for divesting ourselves of all disturbing physical influences during meditation.

Nor shall we one day be able to enjoy the sudden cessation of all bodily feelings. Quite wrong! In meditation there are no surprises; and those who expect them in any shape or form will always be disappointed; either because there will be no surprises at all, or if they should experience unexpected psychical phenomena, their very surprise will ensure that there will be no recurrence. However, this happens so rarely that I regret mentioning it at all.

Our relationship to our environment, too, changes so naturally and so organically that only when we look very carefully can we see that our life has· become a little more evened out. Basically we shall be able to say no more than that our world is really beginning to become a little more reasonable.

A wise student of human weaknesses once said with great humour:

"I have good reason to be satisfied with my father. When I was seven years old his ideas were quite unreasonable. Ten years later he had learned a little more, the older I got, the more reasonable he became, and today I can even listen to what he says."

We always believe that the world changes. If we would but learn that it is only our attitude towards it which constantly changes!

And similarly, our "bodily sensations" will not suddenly stop—we shall only become less sensitive to disturbing influences.

And where does this take place? Not on the surface, but in the very middle, in the nervous centre.

Thus, we shall not have become "insensitive", but we shall merely have acquired other "interests". Our attention, which is usually so busily occupied with physical comfort, will devote itself to other and much more important things; we shall no longer be distracted while thinking; indeed, while thinking we shall even forget that we have a body at all, and we shall become all thought (let us call it this for the present). Since the body no longer forces itself on our consciousness because of our completely relaxed posture and immobility which have both become habit during the preparatory exercises, we get the distinct feeling that it isn't there at all. We can now await results with confidence.

However, until we do obtain them, many things will disturb us, and these cannot be ignored completely: feeling hot or cold, a desire to cough, toothache, fatigue, etc. All these can be "forgotten" but never by force.

Feeling cold is no worse than feeling hot, but cold can be

prevented by blankets and warm clothes. In the beginning a strong cough or a toothache will put a stop to all meditation for the whole duration of the complaint: similarly, if we always feel tired just at the chosen time, it is advisable to change the hour, or even to do a special exercise to rouse us beforehand, as is generally done by many Asiatic schools of meditation.

In the Japanese Zen-Monasteries this exercise often takes the form of a run. If we have not the necessary space, we can do gymnastic exercises instead, but even better, we can use the following breathing exercise of Hatha-Yoga. This is most beneficial, for it increases the oxygen content of the blood evenly and naturally, and not only removes fatigue but also improves our general physical state:

Remain in the position of meditation which you have already assumed. Thumb and third finger of the right hand are placed on the right and left nostril respectively, while the second and first fingers are loosely placed on top of the nose. The little finger lies alongside the third finger. The tips of the thumb and the third finger are only applied so lightly that there is no definite pressure, but so that breathing can, nevertheless, be stopped.

Now, the left nostril is half opened so that we can inhale without difficulty; immediately after inhalation it is closed again, the right nostril is opened half-way, and we exhale equally easily. We inhale again through the same *right* nostril (half opened), and exhale through the *left* one (again half opened).

Generally it is sufficient to do this about ten times. Here, as in everything else, exaggeration can lead to very serious damage.

It must be emphasized that this breathing exercise may only be performed on an untaxed stomach, and with the upper part of the body held straight. Those who have a weak heart should only try this kind of exercise under the supervision of a specialist, and if none is at hand, they should rather shift the time of meditation. We must be patient with our short-comings, and must be magnanimous enough to let them be from time to time, ourselves to remain the stronger. If only we keep both them, and our firm resolve to vanquish them, in mind, then we shall automatically approach the goal without becoming

F

ascetics, self-torturers. This would only turn meditation into a sheer hell.

This constant keeping in mind characterizes the second and probably the most important condition of meditation, its mental starting-point—concentration.

No one needs to be told what concentration is; but not everyone can master it.

Concentration is the only and the unfailing portal to success, to every success in life. And if we have said just this of meditation, then we can only conclude that it is absolutely the same as concentration but on a higher level. For concentration does not only mean "attention" but penetration into things and processes. If we concentrate on our work, it simply means that we have all the necessary facts at our disposal, and that we are capable of surveying and mastering them. It means that we clearly recognize the situation, its circumstances and requirements, and that all that is irrelevant is completely pushed aside.

Concentration means gathering the essential; to be concentrated means to be essential.

It is just the same with "inner" concentration; if we constantly bear our short-comings in mind, and if we try to tear the veil of inessentials from them, they become clearer to us than if we take them as given. We must dig at their roots until they perish.

If we are to concentrate on something, this does not mean at all that we must dig ourselves into it desperately. Concentration has nothing to do with effort and means no more than a conscious limitation of the field of attention.

Thus, it was a custom in ancient India for all archers to meet their masters and to compete with them. A wooden bird was placed on a high pole and whoever managed to pierce the eye of the bird with his arrow was declared the victor.

The marksmen stood in a row, and in order to avoid any misunderstandings about the aim, everyone was asked what he thought his aim was, before his turn came.

All answered faithfully: "A bird." Only Arjuna, a wise youth, said:

"I see the eye of the bird."

Arjuna emerged victorious from the match.

It is not only undistracted attention which is decisive here, but what we may almost call a mysterious way of penetrating into the nature of things.

Thus Gilbert Highet[1] tells us of his extremely significant meeting with his teacher Louis Agassiz, the great Swiss natural scientist, a man who—as Highet says—could see things which other people did not:

"In front of me on the table there stood a flat bowl, and Agassiz brought me a small fish with the instruction to study it, and not to speak to anybody about it under any circumstances, or to read up anything on the subject.

'Try to find out what you can,' he said, 'but please, without damaging the animal. When I think that you are ready, I shall examine you.'

After an hour I thought that I had found out everything there was to discover and I was keen on giving my report, and on getting a further assignment. But Agassiz—although constantly within calling distance—didn't bother with me the whole day long, nor on the next day and the day after that. I saw, however, that he watched me carefully.

Thus I renewed my labours; and in the course of a hundred hours I had done about a hundred times more than I had thought possible at the beginning.

I was now full of expectations that I should be allowed to display my new-won knowledge to the master, but still he only bade me a friendly 'good morning', and no more. Finally, on the seventh day came the question:

'Well?'—and while he sat at the corner of my table smoking a cigar, I gave an account of my discoveries. After I had delivered a lecture lasting some hours, he jumped up from the table, made ready to go and said:

'This is a mere nothing.'

"It was clear that all he wanted was to test my endurance, and that spurred me on. I went to work again, destroyed my first results, and after a further week of ten hours' work daily, I had results which more than astonished me, and which satisfied him."

[1] Gilbert Highet: *The Art of Teaching* (Knopf, N.Y.).

I think we are better judges of whether Agassiz merely wanted to test his pupil's endurance, or if he did not perhaps read a more important meaning into the task. Here we find everything that can be said about practical concentration; concentration on the process, looking at it carefully time after time, and identification with its essence (all this can only be experienced).

If two men are each placed on a lonely island, and if one were given a comprehensive library of Western philosophy, and the other only one single wise book—the first one is likely to become a learned man in time, the second, however, a sage.

Concentration means occupying oneself with one object *exclusively*; so exclusively that even the intention to concentrate is forgotten.

The housewife who concentrates on her work will never drop a plate, will do her housework more quickly and more thoroughly, and will never try to excuse herself by saying that "what I lack in brain, I make up for in brawn".

Certainly it is possible to do two things at the same time, but with this we do not do twice as much, but merely do twice half the work, or even less.

Concentration presupposes thinking—*conscious thought* about the demands of the moment.

When we read a book, we do so mainly to recuperate from our *own* thinking. We let ourselves become affected by the thoughts of the author, and see the pictures which *his* thoughts convey to us. We follow his thoughts with our feelings, instead of penetrating his feelings with our thoughts. It is for this reason that the majority of people have a natural aversion to scientific, or apparently scientific, books, for they require, if not independent thought, at least thinking with the author and this pre-supposes concentration on the given subject.

If you are serious about concentration, you will harvest wonderful surprises and further fruits as well.

Choose a scientific book whose contents seem to interest you and read one chapter daily. Then try (after every chapter) to write a short précis of it. This must be done in the manner of Kleist: "When I do not understand a thing, I deliver a lecture on it." Doing this educates us to follow thoughts—to think

logically. Logic, however, means consistency and the correct-
ness of the conclusion can only be tested if we concentrate
on it.

This is true for science, for daily work, for all things in
life: without concentration we have only the form; it is the
depth of our concentration, however, which determines the
depth of our penetration into the essence of the thing.

The enemy of all concentration is prejudice. It tries to
determine the result of concentration in advance. Prejudice
does not think logically. It does not ask why, and remains on
the deceptive surface. The mark of the sage is the lack of
prejudice, that of the fool the lack of thought. Politics uses
the human weakness of inadequate intellectual penetration
and calls this "propaganda". It awakens instinct, but not
reflection. It delivers opinions without allowing them to grow
consistently. It cultivates prejudice in order to make use of it.
That is why, in totalitarian states, "intelligence" is always
quite especially supervised, because dictators particularly have
good reason to fear independent thinking and logic, which
would enable people to see through their doubtful methods.

Only those are truly free who have learned to think.
Thinking, however, pre-supposes concentration, cold-blooded,
i.e. dispassionate reflection on events, taking an independent
stand, being uninfluenced by the opinion of others. This comes
nearest to intuitive thinking which is never deceived. If we
learn to correlate intuitive and calculated thought, we have
all the means of mental freedom at our disposal. Then we shall
be able to shape our lives with our own hands, and we shall
have risen above the mass without becoming dictatorial
towards it.

If you want to free yourself of the opinion of others, you
must understand it better. Those who have their own opinions,
their own mode of thinking, understand the opinions and the
thought of others. And those who have elevated themselves
above the mass begin to recognize the nature of the human
heart and soul—just as a landscape is seen from the top of a
mountain.

The greater our distance from things, the deeper our
penetration. This may be a paradox, but it is nevertheless true.

The newspaper, for instance, relieves us of thought; it is

even a law amongst journalists not to pre-suppose thought in the reader. Those newspapers which best fulfil this condition will always have the greatest circulation. Thus we get our opinions ready-made, and those who dare to have their own, will have to print their own newspapers.

But let us do something unusual:

Let us take a newspaper and from it an event of the day, let us strip it of every commentary—simply take it as a pure event—and try to understand it objectively (perhaps the behaviour of a plaintiff). When we have done this as intensively as Agassiz asked his pupil to observe a fish, and if we do this with all important matters directly or indirectly concerning us, we shall slowly learn:

1. To know what concentration and its results are;
2. To obtain results from meditation most easily;
3. To see the world through different and wiser eyes;
4. To develop abilities and forces which previously we had never even suspected.

Now we know the second requirement: the ability to concentrate (the first one was mastery of the body). But while the mastery of the former had only advantages, the latter has some apparent dangers, and especially when we try to hasten the natural development of concentration by force, because of our impatience.

If we try to master the body by force, then, too, there are disadvantages, but they remain physical, for we do so at the expense of our nerves. If, however, we try to accelerate the ability to concentrate above the organically possible, without having the spiritual resources to cope with the result, then there will occur what the Middle Ages called the revenge of the Spirits for being conjured up unbidden. This is only too natural.

From the store-room of repressions (of which most of us have our share) more comes to the surface than consciousness can digest; and since things only manifest themselves in the environment, it suddenly appears as if we were persecuted by Fate. We are suddenly pushed into difficulties; while there is a feeling that we have become purer, we are, nevertheless, confronted by the indisputable fact that life seems full of new obstacles which we can hardly cope with.

All this has occurred because, while through our deeper understanding (the direct result of meditation) we obtained a clearer comprehension of our inner conditions, and of our inner short-comings, we could not yet mobilize relieving forces.

It is no news that we must not merely recognize our short-comings, but that we must also be ready to remove them, and to work on ourselves in this direction. How to do this correctly is the crux of the whole matter if we wish to achieve anything at all. A thief who, in order to stop stealing has to amputate his fingers, will not cease to be a thief—he will only become a repressed thief.

Thus, the forcing of premature successes in meditation, beyond the natural development simply liberates new or, more frequently, old but repressed inadequacies, which then appear in the most impossible light, never obviously as our own short-comings, but always as external problems which previously appeared insignificant.

This liberating process which in itself is positive, can thus become quite unpleasant; and we can understand why people always recommend a teacher for meditation. However, modern emancipated man is clearly convinced of the necessity of a natural process of growth, and knows at least what is meant by "patience" and "organic development". Just as regular exercises automatically lead to success, so does regular exaggeration automatically lead to inner harm. Here, as in everything else in life.

If we accept the words of Shakespeare: "The fault, dear Brutus, is not in our stars but in ourselves, that we are under-lings", then the cause of all this is quite clear; for then we see that the power of concentration is a real *power*, capable of awakening our innermost soul. Our "innermost soul" is the source of our "Fate"; and all those hidden fate-forming factors —the "Spirits" of the Middle Ages—thus become liberated. They become oppressively active, but if through meditation we have forged the right weapons, we can give them battle with confidence.

Dangers—as we said before—only exist when we are fool-hardy enough to carry out premature experiments with our inner life. True, for this to happen, we require extraordinary curiosity, coupled with tremendous energy; but those who have the wrong ideas and expect grandiose and extraordinary things as the result of forced spiritual measures, are often only too willing victims of these dangers.

Therefore, let us be warned, and let us follow the advice of the ancients, not to do any strenuous concentration *exercises*, but merely to concentrate on what we do and think; to look at things as they really are, to let the essence of things work upon us, to watch everything without prejudice, to learn to think, but not to desire spiritual self-improvement by force.

Meditation is not the impetus which sets our inner pendulum in motion, but the removal of all obstacles which deflect the natural vibration of this pendulum.

Thus both enemies and weapons are mobilized simultaneously, and we do not aimlessly build bridges to unknown shores or arouse those enemies against whom we are defenceless.

THE OBJECTS OF MEDITATION

WHAT happens to my inner self when I meditate? How must I direct my thoughts? Which thoughts are useful and help me on, and which lead me away from the goal?

The simple answer is: all consistently conscious thoughts will help somehow. Since we wish to develop in the most positive direction, we have to plan even the choice of thought.

Let us systematically consider the thought material at our disposal. Thoughts can be divided into two groups:

1. Thoughts about our own personality and its make-up;
2. Thoughts about the influence of the environment.

A more detailed classification of 1 is:

A. Contemplation and discussion of our own body;
B. Contemplation of our own feelings;
C. Contemplation of our own thinking;
D. Contemplation of what we think and feel about.

Before entering into the details of "Thoughts about the influence of the environment" (Group 2), we must be clear about the process of thinking itself, about the seat of the mental process, about the effect of feeling on thought and finally, about the value of the thought content, for otherwise we might easily consider the environment not as a mere content of thought, but as a primary causal factor.

When all this has become clear, then we shall recognize that correct thought is the basis of correct meditation—not, however, a substitute for it, and not its little brother. It is just as necessary a condition as a positive pro-meditative attitude, as the readiness to create mental harmony, the readiness to master the self.

If these thought exercises seem to be very similar to meditation itself, they are, nevertheless, merely preparations. Like

89

all preparations, they have an absolutely positive, effective and unmistakable aim. For instance, we are not polite to those around us because we hope to gain success in meditation, nor do we concentrate on our work simply for this reason, but we act, because *basically* it is better to do so; and everything which is done better also serves meditation. The latter in its turn, will raise us to a more positive potential as soon as we have elevated ourselves from a negative to a more reasonable level. To do all this because of meditation would simply mean that we wish to be rewarded by meditation. Meditation for the sake of results, however, would be an absurdity.

Thus our thought exercises are, in the first place, aids to the achievement of that clarity of thought which is so essential for our lives, and secondly, a transitional step to meditation.

Let us go back to our classification. We must now proceed to a sub-division:

Group A can be divided into:
1. Observation of breathing;
2. Observation of posture;
3. Observation of movement;
4. Observation of the parts of the body;
5. Consideration of the basic elements;
6. Consideration of the impermanence of matter.
Group B is divided into:
7. Consideration of the kinds of feeling.
Group C into:
8. Consideration of the forms of thought.
Group D into:
9. Consideration of the objects of thought (which will be sub-divided further).

If we look carefully, we shall see that in this apparently exhaustive list Group 2 mentioned in the beginning (Thoughts about the influence of the environment) is contained in the Group "Objects of thought" (9), for, if we think of the environment, it becomes no more than an object of thought. Therefore, for purposes of meditation, Group 2 only exists in theory and in practice only when we do not "think consciously", i.e. when we are not concentrated in a self-reflective, but in a self-forgetting way.

These nine classes differ completely in that some of them are the objects of contemplation on special occasions, while others are objects of constant and general attention. General attention requires both posture and movement. What does this mean?

It simply means that we must know what we are doing. Attention to posture (and movement)—we believe—is always there, for after all we do not walk, stand, sit or lie, unconsciously. Although this might be true in general, it becomes a little more difficult if we are asked *how* we walk, stand, sit, or lie, for we have done it so "attentively" that after only one minute we can't for the life of us remember how, for instance, we put our feet down. Apparently we have paid but little attention to those things which we believe to control so perfectly. Indeed, often we do not even know that we have moved at all, let alone why we have done it.

What we have said in an earlier chapter about hands and feet may be applied most beneficially not only to our nervous movements, but to every single movement and what it signifies. This may be thought unnecessarily pedantic, or some theoretical form of thought torture.

Yet do we in fact rub our foreheads consciously during concentrated reflection, as if to help our thoughts along? Equally, do we consciously hide our palms in moments of indecision? Or again hold them out when we want to prove our innocence? Does the body become consciously tense when we are excited? And does our body relax consciously when we feel discouraged?

No, all these movements are completely unconscious, and can be interpreted by the psychologist, the man who understands people. Our unconscious movements and actions betray us to those around us.

Mr. Miller, who for quite some time has been trying to get a word in edgeways, is now fidgeting in his chair. (Does he do that consciously?) Now he interrupts:

"When on earth shall I have the time to think of my work and of my duties? If now I even have to watch my hands, I might just as well straightaway become a Yogi watching himself like a hawk, careful never to make a single false move!"

What makes you think that this is what a Yogi does, Mr.

Miller? And who on earth has told you to do it? Nobody
wants you to watch yourself, but merely to reflect on things
with clear thoughts. At every minute of the day—no matter
what you are doing—you must do it with all your concentration. If you follow this rule, then not only have you a mind free
for self-observation, but also for a hundred and one other
matters of moment.

Why do we laugh at the absent-minded Professor? Because
his thoughts are never with his actions. He is always absorbed
in something else and therefore cannot fulfil the demands of
the moment even to the slightest degree—he becomes a comical
figure.

If my partner in conversation is not conscious (and he is
not if he is *only* occupied with his own thoughts), then it is easy
to entangle him because he can't see what I am getting at.
But it is just the same the other way round. If therefore, we
attend exclusively to the matter in hand, we have a much
greater chance of success from every point of view.

"Very well," Mr. Miller says, "I understand that if it
comes to important negotiations I must be on my guard; but
surely I can't watch every single step I take just as carefully?
Surely, that is utter nonsense!"

No, it isn't nonsense, only unusual. Quite the opposite: it
would be nonsense to be flighty and thoughtless for twenty-
three hours of the day, and then to expect us to concentrate on
demand during the one hour of negotiation or meditation. It
would be nonsense to expect always to know how to act in
decisive moments, if we haven't learned what to do at less-
decisive moments.

We do not want you, Mr. Miller, to turn your thoughts
into puppets, but only to avoid ill-considered and thoughtless
actions. What you do, you must do wholeheartedly.

So much for general (constant) attention to movement
and posture.

The contemplation of breathing, which had first place
on our list, is so important that we shall leave its exhaustive
discussion to the next chapter.

The observation of the parts of the body (especially of the
inner parts) is an exercise in pure meditation, for here we
have no other tool than the power of imagination, and thus

we shall discuss it more fully later on within the framework of the "classical objects" of meditation. The purpose of this exercise is clear: we must learn to see the body as the most material element of our personality. Not in order to despise it as a worthless machine, but in order to assign it the right place within our life process, and not to deify it as the only expression of our beloved ego, at the expense of the more modest, but far more important, components.

We must, and shall here, recognize that the organic body is only the stage on which the many exciting life processes are enacted, but without which there could be no play at all.

Just like a doctor performing a dissection, we shall try to imagine what lies inside this crudely material body, for even though we cannot see what happens within, it is as much a part of us as our hands and feet. Wouldn't it be silly to ignore the existence of these hidden organs? A further step, which only sounds strange as long as we haven't tried it, is the contemplation of Earth, Fire, Water, Air, as the basic elements of our body. Science has left this classification of the human organism Heaven knows how far behind. Our science! If we didn't know it from books, then as far as we are concerned, our body would have empty spaces (air) and be at a certain temperature (fire). The true chemical facts would be completely unknown to us from practical experience. We shall make these "elements" our basis, i.e. we shall contemplate our whole body as only we ourselves can, and as we understand it from *experience*. This, too, is no longer an exercise in attention, but a pure process of meditation.

The same is the case in the next group: thoughts on the impermanence of matter, the search for the true "I". As far as we are concerned, our life on earth ends in the white shroud in which we are buried. What happens after that is hidden in the secret womb of the earth, and passes our understanding. We know this but we do not wish to know it. We close our eyes to it, for only a few—the very strong—can face the ensuing process of disintegration. And this is as it should be, for it is dreadful to have to return to the earth what is hers.

The Hindu burns all his dead, without exception, at the stake.

Although I have an aversion to everything that is dead,

this did not stop me from spending some hours with the "Ghats", less because of the Hindu methods of burial than in order to observe my own reactions.

I am glad I went, for however keen one's phantasy, it can only create self-built images, and even the feelings arising from it are only self-generated if they are not experienced.

If you wish to have a clear inner picture of *what Man is*, go and see a body burnt at the stake!

This is neither horrible, repulsive nor unnatural, it only requires strong nerves. In depth, this experience is comparable only to birth itself.

Here we can see that human life does not end with the closing of the coffin lid, since the ashes speak of something very different from the vague possibility of a strange subterranean existence. The Hindu knows that with the last breath there is demonstrated the division of forces. Functions cease, the earth takes back its own, but all that was capable of love, laughter and tears is already prepared for new loving, laughing and crying. Somewhere else—and this has been so ever since the Creation of the world. We shall know this suddenly and unequivocally.

Let he who says "I am only my body" go to the stake and let him see the flesh go up in flames. Let him see how there the certain conviction is formed that we must look for the *true* "I" elsewhere than in the remaining ashes. For existence and life are no mere functions. In order to *understand* this, however, we need hours of the deepest meditation.

It is wrong of some books on meditation to say that the contemplation of death is not for the Western man. For us it is one of the deepest and purest of experiences, if only we see in death a natural phenomenon, and not what human prejudice has made of it. For where Nature speaks directly, we always experience deeply. There are still some places in the heart which are reached more quickly by truth than by intellectual prejudice.

The contemplation of feelings (Group B) is easier than would appear at first sight.

Feelings can appear to be strong, weak, or apparently absent. They can be joyful, negative or indifferent. They change with every sense impression, but most frequently they are so weak in their expression that they are unnoticed, if we do not watch out for them most carefully.

We can make our feelings an object of constant contemplation, but this assumes a very high degree of thought mastery. It is very useful for occasional concentration, especially when we are concerned with determining who is responsible for our bad mood.

Mr. Miller is always annoyed about the jammed window. Yesterday, too, it jammed but did not make him cross, because yesterday his feelings were definitely positive, just as today they are definitely negative. If he is aware of this he will not blame the window, but his lack of concentration, for once the bad mood has got hold of him, it becomes extremely difficult to remove it simply by concentration—in most cases it is only displaced. The moment that the first signs of negative feelings are noticed early in the morning, the surest remedy is to concentrate on their possible causes, before any second signs appear. I have never experienced a single case in which a bad mood developed after this.

If we make a habit of considering the first negative occurrence on a black day as our own fault, we shall have banished any subsequent misfortunes.

This may sound like magic, but it is simple psychology, and above all, it is successful.

Thought contemplation (Group C) is a little more far-reaching and more complicated, and can equally be the task of constant attention (which here, too, requires a high degree of mastery), of concentration (that, too, is not easy for we are required to concentrate on that which is the essence of non-concentration) as also of meditation; indeed, those will fare best who endeavour to develop all three, for in the Buddhist texts it says quite rightly and instructively: "Thought (citta) creates all distinction between all things" (Kashyapapari-varta 98).

Everything, the shallow and the profound, the logical and the illogical, the important and the trivial, everything springs from thought and is determined and guided by *thought*.

We mean nothing else here than the contemplation of the thought *processes*, or perhaps their essence. In other words, we must know *whether* we are concentrated, *whether* we think without prejudice or not, *whether* thoughts have an evil basis, *whether* they are due to a whim or to calculation, etc. It is a "watching of oneself" in order to "detect", to "transform" and to give warning. And if we discover that in the background there lurks a tendency which we have decided to attack (for everything begins in thought and ends in fiction and not vice versa), then we have done more to fight inner (and outer) evils than is commonly assumed to be the case theoretically.

If, for instance, we are occupied with important work which has to be completed quickly, and if suddenly we catch ourselves doodling, or watching the street-cleaner, then we must not simply recall our thoughts (this is no more than drill), but we must also ask them very seriously why they act in this manner. If we do this, we shall bring our *true* attitude into the open and thus expose our secret desires (this is true education). For it would be evil to delude oneself into believing that one is a very keen worker if in fact, one is not. It gives us a false picture of our potentialities, and makes us very discontentedly perform our duty purely as a duty, while our true talents perish just because we weren't brave enough to face the truth.

The world would have far more geniuses if all men would honestly feel concerned about their natural talents which, after all, cannot be expressed in any other way than in the flow of thought.

However, success does not lie in brooding, in thinking about our own capacity for genius, but in understanding the basis of thought. Not in dreams, in giving our thoughts free rein, but on the contrary—in the knowledge of *why* we think so, *why* we dream, *why* we brood, *why* we lack concentration, do we arrive at results. These results lead to the last group of our considerations of our personality: the consideration of thought objects and their evaluation (Group D).

This too (with varying intensity), may proceed on all three levels: general attention, concentration and meditation. It is the most far-reaching and perhaps the most important group, for by it we form our basic attitude to the world around us. Therefore, we wish to discuss it in a special chapter ("The Philosophy of the Thought Content").

THE OBSERVATION OF BREATHING

BREATHING is very strange: it works automatically (as do the other inner organs), yet we can regulate it consciously. We could live quite well without some organs, and they all function without our being able to control or correct them. Without breathing, however, we cease to live, and although we can end our life by consciously ceasing to breathe, we never use this means when we are tired of living, even though it seems the nearest at hand, but use other methods instead.

Breathing is the only conscious bodily function which, as it were, proceeds before our eyes; no other bodily processes are visible to us and are hardly, if at all, detectable.

For this reason respiration takes special place from every point of view; we shall use it as an aid, and learn to value it.

Above we have spoken of the three forms of observation: general attention, concentration and meditation. The breath is an object of observation which can only be considered under the heading of concentration; and this limitation must be strictly adhered to.

For if one were to make breath an object of general constant attention, and if one were to do this consistently, then suddenly one evening when attention wishes to change into the "non-attention" of sleep, we shall experience choking phenomena, because our breathing will revenge itself for this conscious watchfulness and these new methods. It will automatically stop its work. Again this is the result of forced measures.

The observation of breathing is the ideal means of introducing meditation through concentration, since it is not only advisable but absolutely essential to be concentrated before entering into meditation. Abstract ideas are little suited to this, and external means require a highly volitional, i.e. dynamic effort of attention, thus opposing the very nature of meditation.

Ideally we should observe an object with our eyes closed,

for the visual sense impression although always the most decisive, is unfortunately the one on which we can concentrate least easily. Breathing is the only "concrete" automatic, i.e. constantly active, process which we can observe without any great difficulty and with closed eyes. What is the greatest advantage of this?

We can compare attention to circles about us whose centre is our thought apparatus. The nearer the circle, the greater the concentration; and if the circle should lie within our so-called "I", then practical concentration is at its maximum.

This is proved by the following fact alone: the farther the field of vision, the more objects we can see and thus consciously distinguish. We "observe" these objects, and that part of consciousness which "observes" them is withdrawn from the process of concentration, i.e. concentration is no longer absolute. However, if the eyes are closed, no external sense stimulus is involved, and we have the theoretical possibility of absolute concentration.

Theoretically! What happens practically is that thoughts now become actions because they lack the living pictorial support. They have nothing to concern themselves with, and thus begin to construct from the raw material of received intuitions and impressions, honeycombs of calculation. From them we are likely to reap the questionably sweet mead of decisions. In these processes the dynamics of restlessness lie hidden.

The best way of purifying consciousness is spiritual relaxation, "idle" thought, i.e. the resting-in-itself of the spirit.

"Not thinking" here means "not constructing", not working with thoughts. This is the path to the purest form of thought; to the exclusive occupation of the mind with one single object which then may serve as a symbol of Nature, of life, of the uncreated, uncompended, the one, the absolute.

Breathing symbolizes life, for it is a process unconditioned by matter. It manifests itself in and with substance alone. In experiencing breathing we experience life. We need not seek anything behind it because it can speak to us directly, and through it alone we can obtain answers to the questions: "What is life? What am I?"

The old Indians called the soul "*Atman*" which is the same

word as the German *"Atem"* (breath). This does not mean that
breath is the soul, but it does mean that when you have
understood the essence of breathing, then you have understood
the soul itself. As our breath, so our soul also, as our soul, so—
the "I".

And what "is" breath?

This is the same question and requires the same answer
as the famous poser of children: "Where is the wind when it
is not blowing?"

We laugh at this question, because we are so clever; but
if we should *really* try to give a serious answer, we suddenly
have to stop laughing and we become embarrassed. Children's
questions have the privilege of embarrassing us, because we
have forgotten to ask them ourselves. Nothing is more reasonable than to follow an incomplete answer with a "why?" We
could very well make something like the wind into an object
of meditation, to discover that it is merely a concept without
any real basis in fact, that actually it is nothing but "the motion
of air" which had always been there before; in other words,
that it does not exist at all. But that "wind" is there, is
undeniable. Thus we cannot say of wind that it "is", in the
same way that an object "is", or that it "is not" as a dream-
image "is not".

This can be seen even more clearly in the case of breath;
and if we "suspect" what it is about (this "being" and "not
being" object), then we can answer questions on the soul and
the "I".

What the answers will be depends on how exclusive our
concentration on the object in question is. We do not wish
to fall into the error of most classical and modern books on
meditation which tell the novice beforehand: "You will be
able to discover this and that"—try it yourself and find out
what your own breath has to say to you.

Sit down quietly, close your eyes, breathe, and follow your
breath with attention! You will be well rewarded. But please
remember our example of the fish!

No exercise is recommended more highly, by theoreticians
and practitioners alike, than the observation of breath; and
from the most intellectual to the most mystical there exists
complete unity on the value of breath-observation, since it

involves all realms starting from concentration down to the deepest meditation. Yet there is no danger (or hope) that we shall suddenly be plunged from the observation of breath into a condition of meditation. The path is a long one.

The observation of breathing itself is simple enough and gives proof positive that it is always the simplest things which are the most difficult, a fact which we might already have noticed during our "lying still" exercises. Thus, both these exercises are somehow related, and this is their common importance.

Let us stay awhile, before entering into details, and let us use breathing as the milestone for another short but essential survey.

The absolute conditions for inner (and therefore, also outer) development are:

1. *Physical Conditions*, perfected through the "lying still" exercises;
2. *Mental Conditions*, perfected through general mental attention and through concentration;
3. *Spiritual Conditions*, perfected through meditation (however, we have not got there yet).

We must avoid being weighed down by apparent necessities, by apparently having to think of a hundred and one things. The less weighed down we begin the exercises, the better we have laid their foundations.

Indeed, we shall notice that the essence of the "secret" lies in discarding. First of all we must discard that nervousness which is expressed in physical restlessness, and this will give us an important faculty: that of becoming *physically* independent during concentration. Then we must discard roaming thoughts, and this will lead to the second faculty: that of becoming *mentally* independent, during self-concentration. Only now have we arrived at the beginning of meditation proper, and yet we have achieved so much already, that we could rightly ask: why should we still need meditation?

This question will only be answered when we know what it is that we must discard through meditation, and by what means we may become *spiritually* independent.

Then what is the technical procedure in the observation of breathing? The most important law for concentrated and meditative observation of breathing is:

Only watch breath, do not influence it!

We do not wish to do any breathing exercises, no Hatha-Yoga, no Pranayama; no exercises at all in fact; we wish to do no more than watch our breath coming and going.[1]

Strangely enough, in the beginning this will cause us some discomfort. We shall notice our breath objecting to such inquisitive watchfulness. It will start behaving like a school-girl and will not move naturally any longer. It will become strangely deep, will be clearly noticeable, the blood will get more oxygen through increased respiration, and the heart will beat a little faster. All in all, things will be so strange that the observation of breathing will become a very exciting matter.

If, however, we should feel uncomfortable, then we must give it up with a smile and think of something else for a little while. Breath will acknowledge it with a grateful sigh.

We can repeat the procedure after a few minutes or, in any case during our next exercise, until such time that we can watch as long as we wish without experiencing any difficulties in breathing.

Why does our breathing seem to be obstructed? Is it so in fact?

Oddly enough, yes, without our wanting or feeling it. When we do not watch breath, apparently it seems to be as regular as an automatic bellows. But only apparently so. In fact, the opposite is the case; if left to itself, it is so surprisingly irregular that this merits some discussion and is also most instructive.

We only *think* that we must breathe regularly. Breath itself, however, is regulated by the precise physical requirements of the moment. These in their turn are influenced and determined by the work of the sense organs (amongst others).

Every external impression requires a new inner orientation, and this is done by the psyche which is in direct contact with the organs, especially with the heart. Every inner movement,

[1] The reader will forgive me if I repeat it once more; but it cannot be said often and seriously enough, and it must be stressed: Yoga breathing exercises may produce the most serious damage to health if they are not supervised by an experienced Yoga teacher.

strong or weak, has its physical reaction; and in order to level these reactions, the organs (especially the heart) have to work at different rates.

If breathing (as a connection between outer world and inner function) were a completely uniform bellows without the slightest possibility of change, then the organs themselves would have to level out the difference in the fuel requirements, and our inner functions would differ from moment to moment. Through irregular breathing, however, we obtain just the right amount of oxygen needed by the heart, and so it can work evenly without giving us any physical discomfort.

The more even our psycho-physical impressions, the more even is our breathing; the more lively they are, the more lively is it. If one observes a sleeping person, we can tell by his breathing whether he is dreaming or whether he is in a dreamless, deep sleep.

At the start our observation of breathing is prejudiced, over-interested, and tinged with the false conviction that we must, at all times, breathe peacefully and completely evenly. It is for these reasons that we regulate respiration by force, and since this stimulates it to greater activity (when it proceeds unconsciously it sometimes stops for seconds), the heart has to bear the consequences. This is an interesting fact which even those with heart complaints can test without danger, if only they stop as soon as it becomes unpleasant.

Positive results come more quickly than in the "lying still" exercises. After only a few weeks we shall theoretically be able to watch our breathing without any difficulty, sometimes for hours. In practice we shall hardly be able to do so because our power of concentration, of thinking of breath *alone*, is discouragingly small. In order to learn to concentrate for a longer period of time *at all* without external thoughts destroying the attempt, the observation of breathing offers, if not the only, certainly the best means!

Here is yet another suggestion for purposes of the exercise:

What do you do on the bus early in the morning? I know: First you read the newspaper, then you brood, then you dream, and then you must get off.

Let us change the sequence a little: try, even when standing in a crowded tube or bus, to arrest your thoughts from one stop to the next, and to concentrate on breathing alone. Turn it into a sport! Even if you don't manage between the first two stops, perhaps you will between the next two. Do this until it displeases you. Then you may read your newspaper.

This will probably help you to gain a tremendous distance from the annoying things and events of the day; the more so because soon you will notice that you can extend the exercise over two or three stops. This is a great achievement in itself and will certainly have a hundred and one favourable consequences during the rest of the day.

There are various methods of observing respiration, each one with a significance of its own:

1. Observation of breathing as an independent means of concentration;
2. Observation of the path of the breath within the body;
3. Observation of inhalation and exhalation as bodily functions;
4. Observation of breathing as a process.

These four methods of observation differ completely from one another, both in procedure and in results. It is therefore advisable to be guided by practical experience and to observe the given sequence. We shall discuss the best way of doing so.

Experience shows that the first exercise is the easiest and the most pleasant. With this exercise the breath must be watched as if it were a rosary, a sequence of pearls which have to be counted and no more. Form, depth, duration, path, etc., of each breath is completely unimportant.

Counting, however, proceeds *pictorially*, i.e. as soon as breathing begins, a luminous number has to rise before our (closed) eyes. For the duration of the breath which proceeds in and out as peacefully as in sleep, we must be able to see the number in front of us, and this so clearly and pictorially that we notice every detail of its form (whether it is plastic, its colour, its size, its shape down to the finest detail). The weaker the picture of the number, the smaller the concentration, and this will always occur with some numbers. Thus, we must count up to ten, where the ten is represented by a zero. Then we start again.

As is the case in all other exercises, this one, too, is only done for as long as it gives us pleasure. Rather than become nervous we must stop. Success will come by itself.

This exercise requires the participation of a large part of our inner self, so that the danger of distraction is relatively little, but naturally by no means excluded.

Similarly with the next exercise—the observation of the path which the breath follows within our bodies. We all know only too well that there are objective limits to this endeavour; nonetheless we shall try it, for it is less the result of observation which is important than the result of our efforts; we do not wish to forget that breathing itself is not as important as its present task—i.e. to become an aid to concentration.

Indeed, just *because* it is so extremely difficult to follow the path of the breath attentively—how it streams through the nose, the nasal cavity, the throat, the pharynx, the bronchi, into the lungs, and how it streams out again along the same path, yes, even how with every drawing of breath, something strangely refreshing flows into all parts of our body—it is an excellent aid to concentration.

This exercise is definitely more difficult than the previous one, and therefore it is best carried out only when the first exercise can proceed with some degree of concentration.

The third exercise is technically more simple than the previous one, because the object of observation is more easily understood; it is no more than the renunciation of concentrated thought in favour of quiet observation, and here lies the danger, for when thought is not strictly disciplined it may easily wander.

Here we only consider the physical *feeling* produced in the nasal cavities by the breath as it streams in and out. Thus, we do not observe the process of breathing, nor any other affected parts of the body, but only the edges of the nasal passages— nothing else. This is a step backwards as far as the amount of inner effort is concerned, but is decisive progress in the direction of our goal—meditation.

Do not work your way through this exercise too quickly; and if you cannot feel at ease for at least five breaths, then you

THE OBSERVATION OF BREATHING

must not yet proceed to the next, but must return to the previous exercise. There is no need to hurry.

The last of these exercises will only be mentioned very briefly because essentially it is part of meditation itself. In order to understand it fully, we must first have mastered the realm of concentration—not only its description, but mainly its practice.

This observation of breathing as a process is a form of attention without the intervention of active thought, owing to the complete pacification of pictorial thinking.

Thinking without pictures and concepts is pure meditation and will not be discussed for the time being, since we cannot understand it as yet. If we mention the fourth exercise all the same, we only do so because concentration is not unrelated to meditation, but is its true source.

In the course of this exercise, consciousness is more and more separated from pictorial and conceptual thinking, mental activity ceases more and more so that concentration, i.e. attention, begins to become more centralized and independent when we reach the fourth group (Observation of breathing as a process).

Until this is attained, however, our original impatience— this most dynamic of all inner processes—must have abated; and for many months we shall do no more than let the luminous numbers rise up before us. Our inherited characteristics determine the duration of this exercise even before the start, by an iron law of Nature.

Only when we are sincerely determined to stick to the first exercise can we count on soon being ready for the second. Some do so after months, some after weeks, but some only after decades.

Certainly, the intelligent person will find things much more difficult than the less intelligent; but everyone with patience and perseverance will get there sooner or later.

Swami Vivekananda, the well-known Hindu missionary, tells the following beautiful legend in his book *Raja-Yoga.*

The holy Narada was travelling through India. There he saw a penitent who was in deep meditation, and who had battled so long and so hard for deliverance that the ants had built a great hill around him—he had been sitting motionless for years.

"Where are you going?" he asked the holy Narada.

"I'm going to Heaven," he answered.

"Would you please ask God when I can count on my deliverance?" the penitent asked.

A little later, the holy Narada met another man who was happy and in high spirits, did not punish his body, and believed he did enough when he fulfilled his duty with a pure heart. He, too, asked the holy man where he was going.

"When you go to Heaven please ask God when he will deliver me. I would so much like to know!"

Many years had passed when the holy Narada returned along the same way.

"Did you ask God?" the ascetic demanded of him.

"Oh, yes," the holy man replied, "you will be reborn four times more, and then you will have reached the end."

The man began to complain and to cry:

"See how I plague myself," he said, "throughout my whole life! Must I wait another four lives? O, I am at the end of my strength! I am cursed!"

The holy man quietly went along his way and met the second man:

"Well," this one said, "when can I count on my deliverance? Tell me, holy friend!"

The holy man pointed to a mighty tree which reached right up to Heaven:

"Do you see this tree?" he asked, "as many leaves as this tree carries, so many lives will you still have. Then you will be delivered."

The man was jubilant:

"Will it be so soon? Is the end so near? How happy I am! I am most grateful for your message." And his eyes shone with joy.

The holy Narada went on his way with a smile, for he knew: this man had already found his deliverance in this life.

PHILOSOPHY OF THE THOUGHT CONTENT

APART from thought there is no world at all, for "what we do not know does not concern us". As soon as I "know" something I notice it, perceive it, it then belongs to the world; I have to come to terms with it and to include it in the infinite reservoir of my experiences.

Every thought has an intuitive cause within the spirit. It is born "purposefully", its further usefulness is evaluated, and if it is found to serve our purpose, it is then translated into action.

Thus the applications of thought are firstly spiritual, secondly intellectual and thirdly practical.

1. We have an idea.
2. We make a decision about it.
3. We translate the decision into action.

This is how it all looks to our mind:

1. The thought is born, without either picture or concept, as a purely intuitive impression, and at that moment it is pure.
2. The mental process of assimilating this pure thought hardens it into a concept.
3. The thought is given a pictorial form so that it can be fitted into the realm of our experience of the world around us. This no longer contains any representation of the true content of the thought. We remain with only a pictorial symbol of the thought, which is no more the depth of the thought itself than a picture of the life of the person it portrays.

Of course, this does not mean that these processes are unnatural. On the contrary, life would be impossible without them.

Nevertheless, the reflection in the mirror must not be confused with the original. Goethe says in *Faust*: "All life is but a colourful reflection", and all we wish to do is to under-

stand the source of the reflection, the true light, the origins of
soul and life, indeed, the Cosmos, how they express themselves
in us and through us, and how they make up our existence,
our picture of the world and of ourselves.

All this is not meant to influence our ideas of God and
Eternity, and has nothing to do with religion, for we do not
wish to create a new heaven for anybody but only to turn his
old ways of thinking towards himself. "To think more consciously!" must be our motto, not "to believe more critically!"
For, as we said at the beginning—before we bother with
eternity, we must put our own house in order. Need it be
stressed that if we do so, religious questions will solve themselves, and indeed assume a greater significance?

We have dealt with this question of the basis of thought
and of its resultant conscious pictures in order to investigate
the psychological potentialities for meditation.

As long as we consider the picture before us, the process of
seeing, and the response in the soul as three *different* things
which are relatively unrelated, we shall confront the world
as a given fact, but our own psyche as something transcendental.
In vain we shall try to find a connection between them beyond
that of servant and master. We shall see the world as a primary
influence and the psyche merely as its receptive victim. This
way we should not make any progress.

It is quite false for us to consider ourselves as worms exclusively created for the purpose of being trodden on. We shall
continue to do so, however, as long as we accept the mere
surface of the thought image as the real thing, deny its psychical
basis, and dismiss demonstrable facts as mere accidents, or as
false demonstrations.

It is the basic tenet of modern existentialism that we are
apparently thrown into the world without hope. The truth is,
however, that modern man has completely lost *himself*.

We must make sure of the answer to the following questions:

Do I see the world as it is, or is the world as I see it? Do I
see reality, or is reality only a relative response in my soul?

Our thought is not simply a means whereby we can
contact the world around us, but without thinking, without
consciousness there would be no world at all around us; there
would be no one to tell us about it. Further, there would be

no regrets if we had to renounce this world and its values, since there would be no self-consciousness, no conscious "I" for whose sake we would regret it.

We imagine that everything around us is exactly as we see it; that it couldn't be any different just *because* we see it so. Our dependence on it seems to be a very strict law of Nature, so that the very thought of living without any concepts and, indeed, living more fully, is usually considered as a foolish, speculative and useless theory without any "practical value". Platonic idealism is often cited as an example.

But at this stage we can be compared to a child with so pathological a longing for a rocking-horse that it has no other interests, and could never be tempted by a promise of a 50 per cent dividend. To him the rocking-horse is the ultimate reality, and the large dividend is a useless speculation which *can* have no advantages, since the child's mental capacity cannot grasp the "higher facts". Nor will the lonely old man at the approach of death see anything exciting in doing good business; for him it will be no more than a ridiculous rocking-horse, useless at the moment of final decision.

Thus all three—the child, the man and the old one—are on entirely different levels of existence and have different ways of looking at things. Everyone believes that *he* alone has the correct idea of the world, and he is quite right—as far as his *momentary* requirements are concerned. It is not he who has passed a certain age limit who ceases to be a child, but he who has outgrown the ideas and needs of childhood.

Only the capacity of the mind can decide when we have reached this stage. What lies behind us, what we have consciously disregarded and outgrown (like the rocking-horse), has suddenly become ridiculous. What lies in front of us we cannot say—it is an unknown world which has absolutely nothing to do with the demands that life makes on us *at the moment*.

From all these examples we see that we can look at the world with different eyes, without, however, changing the world itself.

Those who are aware of this must surely ask themselves logically: "On what do our constantly changing desires depend?"

Well, in the first place we shouldn't have them *at all* were we sages or saints, who are well known to be above all desires.

Why that is so we cannot understand as yet; but *that* it is so, has long been known. To be quite frank, we all lack wisdom.

When wisdom is *entirely* lacking, then we are the ailing servants of our endless desires, we think of nothing but them, plague ourselves till we have satisfied them, only to find that new desires are born, and so *ad infinitum*. This explains why the sage is happy and contented, while the fool rushes about from morning till night with a nervous frown, trying to increase his possessions.

We said it before: it is wisdom which is the measure of consciousness, and consciousness behaves differently towards those things it wants to own and to those which leave it indifferent.

Our picture of the world around us is not determined by it considered as a whole, but only by the degree of our dependence on the *individual parts* which go to make up the whole.

Thus, when we do ask about the absolute value of the world around, then the answer can only be another question: "What is this world around us composed of?"

We must analyse once more:

Every sense organ (vision, hearing, smelling, taste, tactual feeling) represents—from the point of view of desire—a world in itself. Nevertheless, we shall pass over this sub-division for the moment.

We simply perceive with one of our sense organs. What does "perceiving" mean?

1. The contact of one of these sense organs with the object;
2. The sensation which is created through this contact;
3. The registration of the sensation;
4. The (positive, negative or indifferent) attitude towards the object perceived;
5. The mental grasping of the object;
6. The psychical, unconscious process;
7. The inclusion of the picture of the object in the storehouse of experience.

These seven processes represent an almost immeasurably short, but typical, moment of consciousness abstracted from a constant process.

They are found in every step of meditation; and all this

already proves that meditation, indeed, even the deepest, has nothing to do with "ecstasy" or "hypnosis", which are simply states in which the processes have been arrested at one stage or another.

Since these seven processes belong both to the disorientated "consciousness of everyday life" and to the deepest concentrated meditation, we must look for the distinction elsewhere.

It is found by investigating:

1. *How* this seven-fold process takes place;
2. What *additional* factors are at work.

Buddhist psychology of the Abhidharma differentiates with regard to 2:

1. 19 factors representing the basic elements of wisdom;
2. 14 factors of negative character which include all human short-comings and which impede wisdom;
3. 6 active factors of will;
4. 3 chief factors of active morals;
5. 2 factors which express our immediate spiritual participation;
6. Reason as the basic distinguishing mark of *homo sapiens*, of "the reasonable being", of man in general.[1]

In the last chapter of the appendix we shall have something to say about the psychology of Christian Mystics. In principle it is rather similar, if not as far-reaching.

The seven processes belong—as we have said above—to everyday consciousness; the other forty-five factors can be found in the most various combinations (although never all

[1] The factors enumerated above are called:
1. Faith (in the chosen way of salvation), mental clarity, morality, sensitivity, lack of avarice, lack of hate, spiritual equilibrium, harmony of psychical elements, elasticity of consciousness, empathy of psychical elements, empathy of consciousness, activity of the psychical elements, motility of consciousness, right orientation of the psychical elements, right orientation of consciousness, activity of consciousness.
2. Delusions, shamelessness, lack of scruples, distraction, avarice, wrong intentions, pride, hatred, envy, salfishness, self-torture (qualms of conscience), laziness, slackness, lack of clarity in thought expressed as doubt in the chosen way of salvation.
3. Stimulation, consideration, decisiveness, energy, interest, desire to put into action.
4. Right speech, right action, right way of life.
5. Compassion and the ability to share the joy of others.
6. Reasonableness.

together). A man's character may be evaluated by how many of the fourteen negative factors have gone into his make-up, and how strongly they are represented there.

Meditation can now begin. By means of the preparatory exercises we have created a form of consciousness which may serve as a stepping-stone, and we have:

1. The presence of seven factors of conscious observation;
2. The presence of six active factors of will;
3. The negative factors are pacified so that they no longer manifest themselves, at least not during meditation itself;
4. The presence, in principle, of wisdom. This, however, is not an *active process*, but only a potential or factual condition;
5. The three chief factors of active morals are not active here but are potentially present in the previous group;
6. The two factors of immediately spiritual participation are also inactive, but are potentially present in Group 4;
7. Reason is present as a static, passive factor.

Now, the farther we go towards deep meditation, i.e. in the direction of absolute concentration free of any illusions, the more do the *active* elements recede, so that finally only positive and *passively receptive* factors remain. There is no longer any action on the part of those elements of consciousness which are active, i.e. prejudiced in themselves, and which could cloud our vision.

If we look at the practical consequences of this scholastic classification, we see that in the ideal state of meditation:

1. The seven elements of conscious activity are without any hidden moral or volitional values, but are purely functional;
2. The nineteen potential or factual, but in any case, only passively receptive and (in terms of our final goal), positive factors are functionally inactive, and merely serve as standards for the functioning of consciousness;
3. Reason is neither functional nor value-judging, but merely orders events.

4. Those active remnants of consciousness somehow act as the motor preserving the condition of meditation. The higher the degree of meditation, the fewer of these remnants remain, so that the highest meditation is a pure state of conscious clarity beyond the dynamics of logical conclusions.

To simplify even further, we must have for meditation:

1. The natural functions of consciousness;
2. Our momentary character;
3. Reason;
4. The functions of the will which drive us on.

These factors determine:

1. *What* we see, hear, smell, taste, feel and think;
2. *How* we feel it (pleasant, unpleasant or indifferent);
3. *That* we recognize and judge it;
4. *To what use* we put it.

The motor factors are old acquaintances of ours, for they represent the following drives which are so essential in the beginning:

1. Stimulation to meditation (through the certain conviction of the usefulness of higher development);
2. The consideration of the path to be taken, or the control of this path;
3. The will-power to strive constantly towards an aim;
4. Energy to persist;
5. Interest in oneself and the task;
6. The will to realize, not so much the path (meditation) as the goal (higher development or salvation).

We still want to find out how and why these active elements of the will recede, or rather how they change into *conditions* of consciousness.

1. Recedes as soon as the conviction is won that the path which we have taken is the right one;
2. Recedes as soon as we clearly recognize the path that we have to take;

H

3. Recedes as soon as the aim has assumed lasting value;
4. Recedes as soon as the striving has become a habit;
5. Recedes as soon as we have penetrated to our core (concentration) and to the core of the task (meditation);
6. Recedes as soon as the first step of the aim (fourth degree of deep meditation) is reached.

Through concentrated thought we rise above active thought into the realm of reflection. Unconcentrated thought is tinged with prejudice and thus with negative characteristics. Only when we have shed them does purity begin, only when we transcend dynamics shall we feel the fresh wind of the Absolute. This is neither magical nor mystical; but just as the fish of Louis Agassiz suddenly became more than a mere surface, and just as our prejudices and die-hard opinions veil a host of truths, so does every object of meditation show us another and a much profounder face.

Concentration leads thought towards deeper vision. In this we shall find the beginning of a strange process where we face nothing but material facts, and yet, somehow, feel sobered. This is the moment when prejudice and bias step into the background, when our pre-conceived picture of the object resolves, and only facts remain.

With this, thought is pacified; it is no longer jolted from the store-house of prejudice, and slowly steps out of its accustomed course. Now there begins that pure and immediate experience which is known to us already from the deep enjoyment of art—which, too, does not ask for form, picture and concept, but only requires experience. Every forced conscious striving, every active wish would not only destroy this experience, it would not let it arise in the first place, even if we were ready for concentration. Every *act of will* which leads one step beyond this will only prevent the expected result. For what lies on the heights of this "yonder" can only be reached by a "leaving behind", and is thus not only beyond all will, but beyond all words.

THE CLASSICAL OBJECTS OF MEDITATION

I SHALL now give a long list of objects of meditation which, for various reasons, are thought to be especially beneficial. However, such a list can never be exhaustive, nor is it needed at all since it is not the *number* of objects which is important, but the *intensity* with which we regard each one of them.

There is nothing against choosing a match-box, a handkerchief or a pencil as an object of meditation, and no reason why, after a few weeks, we should not fare just as Agassiz's pupil. Certain objects, however, are especially favourable, and what has proved to be beneficial to many generations may have favourable psychological consequences, even today.

Note well: Consequences! For we are not concerned with the objects themselves, but only with their usefulness in meditation.[1]

The choice of the right object is more important than the questionable ambition to have "meditated upon" as many objects as possible. Indeed, those who can meditate upon one object for some years will invariably be better off than those with many objects. After all that has been said, it is not necessary to give any reason for this. Further, those who attain their goal by means of a unique object will have gained so much in wisdom that they will know spontaneously how to choose and act in the future.

There can be no therapy without diagnosis, no development without clear recognition of what is underdeveloped. Those capable of turning the preparatory exercises into an education for concentration, and then developing the latter to its peak, to meditation, will already have discovered so many of their inner needs and short-comings that they will have no difficulty in choosing from the many objects at hand those which are best and most beneficial.

We shall not simply accept that the traditionally proven

[1] In the recognition of this fact lies the difference between Buddhist and Christian meditation.

objects are some mysterious sort of medicine (for this could easily lead to a form of spiritual obscurantism, or ill-founded mysticism), but we shall investigate their psychological origins, the better to understand them.[1]

I do not wish to leave the choice unconditionally to the meditator and to what (for the moment) must be his whims, since it is always a comforting feeling to know that "what we do" is right. The inner certainty of being on the right path is an essential condition for meditation.

The objects which we shall discuss can be divided into six groups: three groups of ten objects each, one group of four objects, one group of two objects, and one somewhat special group.

The first group of ten is of a material nature, and refers to the constituents of every form of matter. At first sight this group appears incomprehensible, and we could easily mistake it for an aid to self-hypnosis. This is not the case at all, and we shall soon see what the true facts are.

Let us look at the ten objects of the first group:

1. Earth (in the form of a heap of sand).
2. Water (a bowl full).
3. Air (in the sensation at the surface of the skin).
4. Fire (the flame of a candle).
5. A small round disc of blue colour.
6. A small round disc of yellow colour.
7. A small round disc of red colour.
8. A small round disc of white colour.
9. Light (falling through a small hole into a dark room).
10. Space (the open, but finite Heavenly Vault).

Not only the later texts of the southern Buddhists, but even their modern exponents show how little they know of the applications of these so-called kasinas. It is true that these are often mentioned in the writings, but their meaning has been forgotten; and they are used haphazardly. However, this is by no means planned meditation, and the result (if there is one at all), is mostly of a self-hypnotic kind. This is diametrically opposed to the true aim of meditation.

[1] This consideration too, is a significant difference between Buddhism and the mystical expressions of all other religions.

The meaning of these kasinas is very simple and, for purposes of meditation, very practical.

Earth, water, fire and air are the famous "four elements" which, even today, indicate *the* forms of which matter is constituted: solid, liquid or gaseous and finally combining or changing from one form into the other—combustion. We found previously that we can only perceive matter in one of these forms.

Thus, these "four elements" are the only perceivable forms of matter. For direct perception there "exists" no other form.

Blue, yellow, red and white are not only the main colours of our conceptual world, but also those of the spectrum.[1] All visual perception presupposes light, just as space is the basic condition of form in general.

Thus, these ten kasinas represent the basic elements of our visual perception in a practical and understandable way; here there is everything in which "form" can manifest itself.

The first four represent solidity, the second four colour, and the last two are conditions of perception.

This is probably inadequate for scientific analysis, but it must be stressed that we do not perceive analytically.

Without exception, everything surrounding us can be built up from these ten basic elements. What is the rest?— merely appearance, composition and form. These, however, are later and further objects of meditation.

Suppose we have now chosen a material object of meditation, sooner or later, while scrutinizing the object more thoroughly with our mind, we shall be able to resolve it into the above elements, and say:

"I see an object in front of me. In order to discover its true essence I must dissect it into its components. I must free myself from the many-sidedness of the objects, and must take only a *single* one of its elements as an object of meditation."

Whatever the element chosen, it can be found in our list, although sometimes a further resolution may become necessary.

These elements are, of course, no absolute values in themselves, but in their essence they are free of appearance and

[1] See also the *Colour Pyramid* of J. H Lambert (1772) with the same "basic colours".

form. What we see in them leads to an immediate understanding of their absolute origin, without the confusion created
by pictures and far-fetched inter-connected concepts.

This is clearly proven by the great difficulty we have in
answering the questions: what is solid? what is fire? What is
colour? what is light? what is space?

The answer is simple when we merely repeat what we have
learned from books; but it is almost impossible when we wish
to speak from our own experience. This is not only true in the
case of these questions. For the truths of science—right though
they may be—are mere prejudices as long as they have not
been *experienced by ourselves*.

This is difficult to achieve; but nevertheless possible in
just the same intuitive manner in which it was experienced and
recorded two or three thousand years ago. Not by magic, but
by clear understanding, by clear concentrated thought, and by
that absolute vision which is not *free* of thought, but *freed* from
thought.

Who can penetrate form with form? He who wants to cut
glass needs a diamond.

The second group of ten must be treated with great care
if we wish to derive the greatest possible benefit from them.
It is the so-called contemplation of corpses, in ten different
stages of decay. Well—we have spoken of this before—the
Occidental has a different attitude to the dead body from the
Oriental, and from the Hindu especially; and we cannot
safely ignore this. On the other hand, we must be considerate in
our criticism; for, before accusing those who choose these
decaying and crumbling parts of the corpse as objects of
meditation of bad taste or even worse (as we often do thought-
lessly), we should think of the doctor whose blessed work involves just such "bad taste". Though this may shake us to our
very core, it is nevertheless a natural phenomenon and those
who do not wish to see it (nobody will blame them), should
not be blind to such eternal facts.

The "contemplation of corpses" is less for the purpose of
realizing that after death everything must decay, but rather
to show the exact opposite: that what decays, cannot possibly
be *everything*. It is a contribution to "Man know thyself" rather
than a *memento mori*!

We do not want to enter into theoretical discussions here, as in any case it is only the physicians amongst us who could practise this kind of meditation; and phantasy-meditation would be senseless since its results could not correspond to true corpse meditation. Even effigies would by no means fulfil the purpose.

But perhaps all this is to the good, for since on Asiatic fields of carnage I have seen the pitiless alternatives of the consistent meditation of corpses—sanctity or madness—I know that just here it is only the greatest of care and the wisest inner direction by a great teacher which can lead to positive results.

There are teachers of meditation (especially in the South Buddhistic school), who use the contemplation of corpses as a proof of the fact that all beauty is skin deep, and that it passes away with the process of decay. There are even whole textbooks of meditation which try to make this point. Without too much discussion, we simply want to contend:

It is certainly not beauty which decays, but only that which served as its vessel. Beauty is immortal as long as there is but one being left to experience it. It is not found in decaying matter, which is but a *transmitter* of beauty, but only where it is immortal: in our own hearts.

The third group of ten is a treasure house of abstract objects, which are all of the strongest psychological and character-forming value.

I—BUDDHA

We have already spoken of the value of a small figure of this material embodiment of self-reflection. Whether we are Christians or Buddhists, we simply consider the Buddha as a symbol of all we mean to reach through meditation, and connected ways of developing.

In choosing him as an object of meditation, we choose ourselves simultaneously, i.e. *that* "ourselves" which is our goal, when cleansed of all present faults. This only the Buddha can symbolize.

He is the answer to the question—what is the goal of meditation? All that is "form" in his statue is insignificant. What matters is the effect. Perhaps peace, perhaps a smile, for this peace and this smile will one day fill us; but it will not be the peace, nor the smile of a worthless statue, a worthless body, a worthless work of art. The picture, the body, the work of art will one day decay; the peace and the smile, however, will have become our imperishable possessions. This is the Buddha in us, and meditation will have reached its goal.

2—THE TEACHING OF THE BUDDHA

It is not necessary at this stage—indeed it might even be dangerous—to immerse oneself in great mountains of thick books, and to accumulate knowledge through research. The entire teaching of Buddha can be given in twelve words:

"Avoid what is evil, do what is good, and purify the heart!"

Please do not say: "This is ridiculously little!"—which single one of us can, at the end of his life, say that he has fulfilled these requirements?

"My religion commands just that!" said another.

Certainly! Nobody has said that your religion is "wrong".

All praise to him who says: "These twelve words are much too much all at once. Give me only a part of them!"

He may have them. The first five counsels (not commandments) of the Buddha are:

1. Never kill or damage (even spiritually) a single living being!
2. Do not take what is not yours!
3. Be pure in thoughts, words and deeds!
4. Do not lie.
5. Avoid intoxicants—i.e. things which cloud clear thinking!

And for those who think that they can easily fulfil these, here is an eight-fold path to deliverance:

1. Right attitude (create a clear picture of the world, of life and of that which you call your "self").
2. Right decision (decide to go along the path which may lead you to your true enlightened self).

3. Right speech (do not create suffering through thought-less words, for he who creates suffering must bear the consequences of such suffering himself).

4. Right acts (act consciously, for only then can you judge whether your actions are good or evil).

5. Right way of life (fulfil the demands of the day with a pure heart! He who howls with the wolves becomes a wolf himself).

6. Right aims (do not aim at things which will create suffering for you or for others. Delusion is short, regrets are long).

7. Right concentration (do not approach things with prejudice, nor with avarice or hatred).

8. Right meditation (truth is deeper than your prejudice can imagine; the recognition of truth means deliverance from suffering which surrounds you everywhere, and which threatens you daily and hourly).

Here we have so deep an object of meditation that our life is hardly long enough to plumb it. He who thinks that this, in any way, contradicts his own religion, must have misunderstood something very fundamentally: either in the teachings of the Buddha, or in his own religion.[1]

3—THE MONASTIC COMMUNITY OF BUDDHA

Here, I grant you, we have a classical object of meditation which cannot be used in its original sense by Western Man,

[1] At this point I must stress that I am not attempting to give a complete idea of the teaching of the Buddha in this book. That would go far beyond the given framework. If here I speak of his doctrine as an object of meditation without going into details, then the reader may consider the following: Buddhism is not a philosophy which primarily contends that it changes the intellectual world picture. It is a practical way of enlightenment which, through morals, wisdom and inner reflection, leads Man back to his true sources, away from avarice, hatred and prejudice. The above-mentioned counsels lead to this directly. What we have said corresponds completely and immediately with the doctrine of Buddha, although I have not used his words. If, however, the given objects of meditation are taken out of their framework and are then considered to be incomprehensible, something basic has been misunderstood. If the connection with the whole is seen, more of the doctrine of Budda has been understood than long dissertations would have permitted. Why did I avoid canonical words? In order to avoid a cult with poorly translated words, and to give instead their hidden meaning, which alone is capable of conveying to us how relevant this wisdom is to our life and times, even if some will persist in calling it strange and "purely Asiatic".

because he fails to grasp it. I should have omitted it completely if it could not be adapted for our purpose at all, i.e. to reflecting on our inner reactions, while thinking of a life completely shut off from the outer world.

"Could I lead the life of a pious hermit? If not, why not?" This question is not meant to prepare us for the life of a monk. But it is often in the strangest questions, that the most significant answers are hidden. Since the life of a monk is the result of consistent inner development (in any case it is meant to be), the answer can tell us many things about what *we* still lack in *our* development, for progress to the point where we *could* lead the life of a hermit if we wanted to or had to.

For a monk does not go to the monastery because he cannot stand the world any longer (woe to him if he does it for this reason!) but only because he is beyond it. It no longer holds him in chains.

We who wish to enjoy the world for a long time yet, have also decided to cast off our chains, for how else could we be happy? Who could, for instance, be happy in marriage while he considers it a form of bondage? Here we have an object of meditation which (let us recall the first chapter) leads us to the question of "possessions" and also to our true attitude towards them.

This group of ten, in its first object (the Buddha) poses the question of our inner "self". In the second object (the doctrine) we have the question of the capacity of the "self". In the third object (the monastic life) we have the question of the attitude of this "self" to the environment (analysed in the first group of ten). In the second group of ten (the contemplation of corpses), it would have been recognized that the body is only of secondary importance in our search for the "self".

Thus, we have a clear sequence which is more useful the more consistently it is observed. We cannot observe it in the theoretically ideal way, but we shall find a path which, although longer, is less dangerous for the soul.

4—MORALS

Suggestions for an irreproachable moral life are found in the first five counsels of Buddha, in parts 3, 4 and 5 of the eight-fold path, but also in the three main elements of active morals, such as "right speech, right action and right living", and in the 52 factors of consciousness investigated in the chapter, "The Philosophy of the Thought Content".

Only the thoughtless will smile when asked:

"*Why* shouldn't you kill, *why* shouldn't you steal?"

If he laughs at so naïve a question, ask him why! He'll soon stop laughing.

There are many answers, but each less satisfactory than the next: "Because it is forbidden by law", "because God punishes it", etc. Why does He punish it? Because it is an evil deed. Why is it an evil deed? What is evil? Are there absolute, generally valid definitions of good and evil?

He who drives himself into a corner by constant questioning, until he can no longer find a reasonable answer to a reasonable question, has arrived at the beginnings of meditation.

To ask somebody else would be wrong; for it would not only delay knowledge, but mislead us. We cannot become wise through the wisdom of others.

Those who maintain without self-enlightenment, that they couldn't kill, steal, lie, etc., are the victims of one of the most dangerous prejudices, for not one of us knows *a priori*, what lies dormant within us. Many of us had to recognize this when, in the horror of war, they were confronted with the fact of a "changed" self. Anyone who has experienced this is more careful with the contention:

"I don't need such moral laws, for in this respect I for one am irreproachable."

Certainly, our dynamic will may be irreproachable. Is it the same in the sphere of our inherited characteristics? If it were so, it would be easy to predict the future life and character of the newly-born.

Those who base "necessity for morals" on the demands of the social order, will certainly find themselves at a dead end; for they forget that such demands can change overnight into their very opposites, when it is a dictator who makes the social laws. In that case—under the guise of moral demands—a whole people can become the victims of the changing whims of a single man.

No, we must try to discover a basic law which is just as

binding for the savage in the jungle as it is for the Pope. This
does not mean "be good!", but "become better!"; it does not
involve "knowledge" but "enlightenment". It is not so much
the "point of view" which is important as the "path of development", not the "*being* free" but the "*becoming* freer'.

Therefore, to "*be* moral" means to be self-satisfied, but
"to *become* more moral" means rising to higher levels.

This law is universally valid.

5—GENEROSITY

Generosity is determined firstly, by the degree of our
dependence on things and secondly, on how much we understand and feel the needs of others.

Generosity determines the measure of our own worth—
either present or to be developed. For—and this we must
accept without comment—the sages of all nations and of all
times have praised generosity as one of the virtues capable of
leading to greatness. Later on, we shall find a very closely
related group (compassion and sharing the joy of others),
where we shall enter more closely into our inner relationship
with our fellow-men.

6—GOD

It is important to be clear about what is understood by
"God". It is obvious that the word itself is insufficient, indeed,
that it can be interpreted in many different ways. Therefore,
we must be clear about the *source of the value of this experience*.
I fully agree with those who will here say indignantly—God
is not a fit subject for thought. For quite sometime I have not
spoken of "thinking", but of "self-elevation above thinking"
through "immediate experience".

Christ said: "Unless ye be as a little child . . ." and He
promised the kingdom of Heaven to "the poor in spirit". To
attain this is the purpose of this book, even though the method
is a little unusual, indeed, even though a "strange" religion
must offer its principles for this purpose.

Here, too, *through thought*, we want to pass *beyond* thinking into experience. Just as in church, just as at a concert, just as in true love. This is God-meditation.

To the naïve Christian this is merely confusing, for he customarily approaches the concept of God with dynamic thought; but this is nothing but the atrophy of his experience of God—an experience completely alien to him. After all, it is unreasonable to expect the average Christian to penetrate the depths of experience, as did the Church Fathers. Certainly he could do so, but in the first place, he would have to be clear about what he understands by "God"—at least on whether he sees Him from the point of view of the prophet, or of the mystic, since the contemporary conception of God is a vague mixture of both. The God-concept plays a predominant role in the consciousness of the greater part of humanity. It may, therefore, neither be ignored nor underestimated. We shall touch upon this theme again in the chapter called "Meditation in Christianity".

7—INNER HARMONY

This is perhaps the most beautiful, the purest and the simplest object of meditation, with comparatively the most far-reaching and yet the most simple experiences. It is the thought which is insolubly connected with the concept of meditation, a thought which must arise whenever we think of meditation, whenever the first preparations for daily meditation have been made.

It is the thought which makes the strongest and the most real contribution to the peace of the world, for it is only the peace in the heart of man himself which is capable of preventing war.

Without this inner peace there would be, and there is, no meditation; and those who have used it throughout life as the *only* object of inner contemplation, have happily fulfilled the demands of their religion—whatever it be.

8—DEATH

Again we meet Death, and again in a different context. At our first meeting we asked him:

"What is the body and what happens to it?" in the contemplation of corpses we asked: "What is the self, and where is it to be found?"

Here we desire the knowledge of *what death is*. Here it shall, and will, lose its horror. This form of meditation is the best antidote against the sorrow produced by the death of a dear friend. Wouldn't it be a wonderful memory to have seen the friend die with a smile, with a wink, with a good-bye?

Meditation of death will give us the certainty that death is only a process of transition.

It would be senseless to waste any words on *what* during meditation becomes a certain conviction, and what would here only appear as cheap consolation from one who is at a distance from the sufferer. However, everyone is a sufferer, since death knocks at everyone's door.

Those who do not wish to probe any deeper, would not even benefit if the great truth of this meditation were described to them. And those also who only enter into this meditation out of curiosity, will be disappointed. Questions about death must not be idle, but must spring from the heart.

Death remains the same, but its picture becomes purer and stranger; it becomes beautiful. A world is revealed which is incomparably more dignified and holier than ours, for in it nothing is sad or gloomy.

9—OBSERVATION OF THE BODY

Observation of the body has been discussed before (p. 90 ff.), but it was not treated deeply since it belongs to pure meditation.

It is easier than one thinks possible to meditate about the inner part of one's body; and those who manage to do so, will soon be able to progress to the meditation of bodily functions.

Meditation of the body is closely related to the meditation of corpses, and is meant to prove that more lies behind the functional process than the mere workings of a first-class motor. In any event, we are convinced of this somehow, but we only *experience* it very rarely, i.e. only when we recognize the "thing behind it" by its effect.

Nevertheless, we want to look for it too; and what we said

by way of preface about concentration on the body, feeling, thinking, etc., becomes more profound here, and leads to a goal which leaves no question and no doubt, for here we are concerned with the riddle of our *own* "self" and our *own* "soul".

10—BREATHING

It is just the same with this last object of the abstract group of ten. Here, too, we have prepared, through concentration, what will now be retraced to its abstract spiritual sources.

Here there is no longer any counting or feeling, but only breathing; we do not think (or do anything else)—we simply breathe. One *knows* that there is breath, but no more thoughts arise, there is only breath—and then not even breath. But this can only be understood by those who have tried it patiently, who have experienced it, who do not expect any miracles, who do not expect anything at all, who have gained the great inner peace.

The next main group of classical objects of meditation consists of only four elements, which are all concerned with our inner attitude to our fellow-men:

1. Goodwill.
2. Compassion for others.
3. Sharing the joy of others.
4. Happy equanimity.

These four are of such infinite importance that we can say that they determine our relations with humanity in general.

I—GOODWILL

What we have here called "goodwill" is actually much more than that: it is a love of living creatures of such depth as is only known to us in mother-love. It is free of every sensual desire which, after all, is nothing else than selfishness. The best mark of *what* this goodwill signifies internally is the well-known formula, usually found at the end of many Buddhist texts: "Peace to all beings!" This is more than a manner of speech—it is something deeply felt. Those who do not feel this deeply every minute of the day, act against the tenets of every religion—their own most of all.

Test your own attitude to it! Go through the list of your enemies and ask yourself if you begrudge happiness to any of them. If this is so, then a change is imperative. For, to wish luck to those we love is hardly a great deed. We must prove ourselves through our enemies; but not by destroying them, but by making them our friends.

This cannot and shall not happen by a displacement of our hatred, and by lying to ourselves, but by considering those as brothers who, too, are the sons of a mother, who are just as hurt by the misfortune (which you wish upon them) as your mother would be by yours.

If your enemy is truly an evil man, he will have (now or later) to suffer for it, and he will feel his suffering no less than you feel yours. But haven't we heard, time after time, how an evil man has found the path to righteousness through the love of others?

How easily man becomes guilty unintentionally, yet without being evil; and how easy is it then to break a staff over him, instead of taking his hand sympathetically and taking him to one's heart. In true despair we are always alone; and if then we cannot find some small corner of our heart to hold on to, we are often lost. Do you know whether your enemy does not despair in his own heart?

But we do not wish to dispense charity magnanimously— we only want to understand our brother. This is something quite different from the unjust charity of the self-satisfied Pharisee.

Those who begin with prejudice are certain to get lost, and to become the victims of their own words.

Goodwill, however, does not begin with goodwill itself; it begins (as all our meditation does) with testing and with questioning. Every question should uncover the good, look for its roots, and (this we know from the factors of consciousness) free us of negative factors, since otherwise there could be no meditation at all, but at most, some form of planned brooding.

This meditation requires nothing else than our willingness to do good!

All questions arising from this (why be good, what is good? How good? How do I find it difficult to be good? etc.) are to be answered during concentration; and if the answers are found there, then we shall choose *them* as objects of meditation; for an intellectual understanding (even if it is concentrated) has by no means *changed* us inside. This can only be done by meditation. The result of this meditation (let us unashamedly call it meditation of the love of Man) is equivalent to the radiant mood of a Sunday morning in spring. It is happiness!

If this happy feeling is not there, then our love for man is not yet genuine.

2—COMPASSION

The second element of our main group cannot be fulfilled without fully developing the previous group. As long as we can still stay: "Thank God, this hasn't happened to *me*," when something unpleasant has happened to somebody else, we shall have far to go. Indeed, only when we say: "I'd rather this had happened to me, for I could have borne it better," have we attained one of the aims of meditation.

Mr. Miller objects, not unexpectedly:

"Now he wants me to worry about the cares of others! As if I didn't have enough of my own!"

Believe me, Mr. Miller, you won't get rid of your worries more quickly by not caring about the unhappiness of your fellow-beings.

Now Mr. Miller will become aggressive:

"Well, will I lessen them by being sorry for everybody?"

Dear Mr. Miller, do you know what it means to have somebody who understands us when we are in pain, in despair and apparently without a way out? Who merely understands? Do you know what it means to *be* such a man oneself? Do you know what consolation, what power, what will to life you are in a position to give through your compassion, through your true *understanding*? And do you know what incredible forces you derive from doing so yourself? No, you do not know it, for otherwise you would not have asked the question. But when

I

you do come to know it, then you will have managed to leave many, indeed an infinite number, of your own cares behind.

Do you ask how that is possible? You will know it when you have made somebody happy through your sympathy.

Never forget that it makes a great deal of difference whether you just moan with somebody, or whether you truly stand by his side.

3—SHARING THE JOY OF OTHERS

Envy is simply being angry at being left out of the happiness of others. We are always willing to share this, but only if we are ready to share their suffering also, will we be able to partake of their good fortune. This is one of the most beautiful laws of nature.

Thus we can see that from human love there arises human compassion, from human compassion, the ability to share the joy of others, and this almost looks like a reward. A reward which, although it is never given away, is nevertheless easily earned.

4—EQUANIMITY

Here we might just as well speak of a "still and considered happiness". "Still" means undisturbable, "considered" means "above any influence", and "happiness" is the best word for that contentment of the wise which rests in itself, and is born out of itself.

Equanimity is never "up in the clouds", nor is it "weary to death". It moved on the path which has ever been known to all the sages of both East and West as the surest and the best path to the goal; the golden mean between too high and too low.

No suffering can shatter this equanimity—yet never will its owner flee from suffering like a coward. He is not lifted up into the clouds—and yet he knows how to value his happiness and how to feel it. Since his life receives a greater share of it than that of the ordinary man, happiness becomes both a source of strength and a shield through which the arrows of suffering can no longer penetrate.

However, equanimity—such as Socrates is reported to have

had—cannot be experienced without human love, without the corresponding compassion, nor yet without joy at the happiness of others.

In meditation, the decision to pass from one group to the next is made at that moment when we have the happy feeling of fulfilment in contemplation. If this is done intellectually, it could only too easily happen that our love of man becomes an advertisement of our own goodness, which changes compassion into a shedding of crocodile tears, the sharing of joy into the sharing of enjoyment, and equanimity into indifference.

One false thought, and positive is changed into negative, and what we want to avoid will now break over us without pity.

This is the danger of the path to salvation. If you try to walk along it deceitfully and ambitiously you will be pitilessly stoned by your own weakness. Then there will be no forgiveness—this is the law of nature.

However, if you walk along it with a pure heart, you will never be disappointed.

After having discussed what may be called our spiritual and mental nourishment, the next main group, consisting of two parts, approaches a new angle of the old problem—our physical nourishment.

Behind this we need not look for a great purpose, nor see in it any great aim, as we did in the last group of four. We only wish to create a clear attitude to this essential process.

Our inner attitude to food needs clarifying—since the importance of nourishment is obviously of the greatest importance to the life-process—many have made a cult of the simple process of eating, and have thus made it a useless end in itself.

One of the greatest achievements of our culture is that it concerns itself with the question of nourishment. Nothing in this is of greater value than the requirement that this natural process should become an act of pleasure. A clean table, a meal prepared with love, a peaceful and happy way of eating— all this is so beautiful, so natural a need, that those who have learned to value it and are then forced to do without, have to sacrifice more than mere etiquette. For cleanliness of physical food is not a bit less important than cleanliness of spiritual and mental food.

This need for cleanliness in the three nourishments has

nothing to do with snobbery, as long as it springs from need rather than from any intellectual principle.

Thoughtfulness in taking in these three forms of nourishment follows the same law. Here, too, as everywhere, it is essential to become absolutely clear "why this is so".

It is commonplace to answer "because it is healthier".

But is a circle only round because it is not square? "Because it is healthier" is a good and correct answer, but it reminds one of medicine and not of natural necessity.

Who, when doing something pleasant, would first ask whether he is "healthy" enough? Thus, we read the newspaper while eating because it is "pleasant" enough though it is not "healthy". It would be "healthy" to chew each bite thirty-two times, but since this is not "pleasant", we only chew it six times, so that we may taste the pleasure of the next bite as soon as possible.

No, we do not demand cleanliness of nourishment and a cult of eating "because it is healthier", but only because somehow its pleasantness makes us happy.

Everybody tries to eat in as pleasant a manner as possible; and those who do it in an unhealthy way, only do so because they have not yet experienced how much more pleasant is a carefully prepared meal than a hasty, unclean one, or else because they look for pleasure in perversity.

Cleanliness is not the privilege of the rich, any more than is thoughtfulness. The happiness of a quiet, thoughtful taking-in of nourishment is a lasting feeling, even if it has no immediate beatific effect.

It is beautifully simple:

We do not think of a thousand and one other things, but concentrate and occupy ourselves only with what is on the plate, on the fork, in the mouth and in the stomach.

Here the *process* of eating, the taking-up of nourishment is chosen as the object of meditation, while the second member of this group is concerned with nourishment as such.

In the latter it is important to become aware of how our physical nourishment is composed of solid and liquid particles, how we overestimate it and get into bondage instead of entering into a wise relationship of reciprocity with it.

Here as everywhere, we look for the deeper meaning. We

will realize that it is not the material which is decisive, indeed, that the material part of physical nourishment is only what the alphabet is to mental nourishment: the carrier of meaning but worthless in itself. It is necessary only as a means.

We shall be faced with the question: *what* is the content? Again we shall realize that the answer is to be found only in our experience. What previously appeared to be a purely physical need will suddenly gain in inner significance with deeper understanding. Our greed, however, will abate.

Thus does eating itself become a part of religion, because religion is not empty piousness, but the experience of life.

In the canonical list of classical meditation objects there now follows the last main group—"abstract deep meditation".

This main group is completely out of place here. It is not meant for those who *want* to immerse themselves in their own spiritual basis, but for those who are already *in it*. Here we should not know what to do with it. In it there are no concepts, no reasonable points of departure, and even if we knew vaguely what it might be about, we should be completely incapable of understanding it from its true content.

Therefore, we must be patient for a little. In the chapter, "Deep Meditation", we shall return to this group, and then we shall be able to understand it, at least to some extent.

THE CHOICE OF OBJECTS

WE have previously stated that the choice of a suitable object ("suitable" in the sense of psychological needs) is one of the most important requirements.

We must be extremely careful in this choice, for it is not only the intellectual but also the psychological (and therefore not obvious) data which are of decisive importance. Thus, the right choice of object is almost a matter for meditation in itself.

It is not possible to give a universal formula, just as a doctor cannot prescribe by rote, but must judge the needs of each individual patient. So we, too, can do no more than give general indications to those who wish to follow the path most suitable for them. We all want different things, yet we shall all recognize our common aim one day. This does not mean that our paths must be identical. Some people have travelled round half the earth to find it, and some live but a stone's throw from it, and do not know it.

Unfortunately the old texts are not always reliable, since most of them were written at a time when extremely keen investigators and commentators placed more value on the written word than on the source of their *own* experience. They relied on the words of the ancients, adding their own opinion, omitting apparent side-issues which, however, were later found to be of great importance. If a sceptical and experienced practitioner looks at these writings today, he will discover much that is wrong, and much that is mere padding. Thus today we can only rely on the texts—however old and reverend —conditionally. And since ours is not critical but absolutely practical work, only that text will do which will help us forward rather than arrest us through its imperfections. Therefore we shall not bother about texts, and if we miss much wisdom on the way, we shall not deny that it is there.[1]

[1] For the expert I wish to say briefly: those passages which I consider questionable are mainly in Buddhagosas *Visuddhimagga* and also in the last part of Anurupphas *Abhidhamatta-Sangaha*, in other words, in texts of the *later* Theravāda. While practical investigation into meditation seems to have been abandoned in them, it revived at that and later times in the countries of the Mahayana. This can be seen from the entire Sutra literature.

If a melancholic person broods over his misery, he is sure to become even more miserable, instead of recognizing his misery as unfounded. He lacks the psychical conditions for this recognition. To gain these he must first have passed through other stages of thought.

Melancholy, as every other wrong attitude, is due to a false mental starting-point. Perhaps the melancholic knows this in theory but he is incapable of creating other thought processes in practice, since logical calculation, though it may lead to intellectual results, never leads to spiritual ones. He knows his difficulties, believes that they are based on a wrong philosophy, but since belief without experience is barren, this dead knowledge is at best, confusing and never useful.

And if we who are "more life-positive" say: "It is silly always to be thinking of death", this may well be due to *our* experience, but not to *his*.

What is experienced can only be shaken by some stronger experience.

Meditation follows the same law as every other therapy: it does not consider it important to remove the effects of false attitudes, or to prevent further false conclusions. It desires to, and must, attack the very roots of these wrong attitudes and, in order to bar new eruptions, it must prepare the ground on which weeds cannot even start to grow because there is no food for them.

The choice of objects must be determined by this consideration. Compared with the time devoted to the contemplation of a chosen object, much too little time and care is usually given to the choice of object itself.

There are men in Asia who reflect on one object for decades; and should we do the same, it is only logical to spend at least one month on choosing the object carefully, and on convincing ourselves of its rightness and importance.

Meditation on death (in all three degrees of contemplation) may only take place after we have, by preliminary meditation, carefully determined if there are no depressive or melancholic traits in our character, or if these are not provoked by preliminary meditation. In any case, it is advisable never to commence any of the three forms of death meditation earlier than after *at least* five years of meditation—in other words, when the great gulf between thinking and experience which we have in the beginning, has lost some of its significance.[1] Further, it is not advisable that the beginner dissect his body mentally, or meditate on abstract concepts, without a previous knowledge of the real value, or that he meditate on the concept of God or the life of a hermit.

Each of these concepts pre-supposes something which we are only too ready to sacrifice to prejudice.

For instance, the common naïve idea of God as formed in the psyche during early childhood, has unconsciously become inadequate for the deeper life of the soul. Thus, we tend to look for objects which might help to widen this naïve idea. However, we shall not get any farther than this archetype, if we do not first pave the way beyond it. This leads to our going round in circles, to our becoming restless, when all the time we know that there is a way. Only we cannot find it because the walls of our psyche are too high.

When looking for a way out of a muddle, we always try to smash through walls, since we believe the exit to be just in the direction in which we are looking. The muddle, however, is not as simple as all that. Only by changing our view can we hope to break free from it.

As long as our idea of God remains a confused one, and our point of view remains childish, we cannot experience freely, or even recognize the true depth known only to the heart, and which the brain merely broods about.

Even the first group of ten which dissects material objects into thickness, colour, appearance and space, and neglects form, the better to demonstrate the elements through which they are expressed, should only be chosen if we are concerned with some material problem, and not if we attach greater weight to spiritual things. The investigator, the scientist, the physicist, the analyst, yes, even the philosopher, all can derive great benefits from these meditations, for the latter will direct thought into such clear and consistent channels and stimulate it so much, that we might say that meditation teaches even the thinker to think almost without thought.

---

[1] One of the most dangerous mistakes made especially by young people is to use the contemplation of corpses for purposes of overcoming sensual greed, with the result that their natural drives are changed into perversity. They forget that the *observation* of corpses is by no means *meditation* of corpses, and force their characters without giving them the chance of maturing naturally.

We shall find to our great surprise that "there is thought" that "a thought process is taking place according to law". In other words, it takes place without the constraining order: I must think now!

The spiritual person may here run the risk of wrongly assuming that some mystical or occult forces might be at work. This would mean destroying what he is so carefully constructing.

Meditation is not meant to develop mysticism, but to remove it; for greater than all mysticism is the clarity of enlightenment.

Those of us who are of a spiritual nature will find sufficient material in the third group of ten, but not all elements of it are equally advisable.

The doctrine of Buddha, i.e. a *practical* moral code, a *practical* way of life, will offer the spiritual person everything he can desire. But meditation of food, too, will be beneficial for him; in short, everything which he can test practically and use in daily life. The symbolic personality of the Buddha himself may only be used in the more developed stage, for we must be completely clear what he symbolizes. Only then is it advisable to grapple with the third member—life in solitude. This question requires more than seriousness, it requires wise maturity.

The quiet contemplation of breath without mental activity is advisable for those whose phantasy is too keen, for the brooders. The choleric, on the other hand, would be better occupied with analysing his own body. He should do so by imagining that he is an outsider looking at himself. The same applies to the materialist, while the religious person must first come to terms with matter, before tackling spiritual questions.

Those who are materialists must first learn to understand the mental content of the spiritual, the brooder the spiritual content of matter, and the spiritual person the mental content of matter. Nothing is *only* material, *only* mental, *only* spiritual, and this fact must and can be recognized, no matter what point of view.[1]

The chosen object is meant to fill our meditative life, but

---

[1] A full analysis of mental, spiritual and physical extremists and their therapy through Yoga is given in my *Der Yogi und der Komödiant*.

not to follow us into our everyday thoughts. It will affect them, but not consciously.

When we shut our meditation chamber after half an hour of contemplation, then we must honestly be able to say:

"It was lovely, but now back to work again!"

This is much better than thinking:

"Ugh, work does not matter, the only important thing is to recognize ourselves more clearly!"

On the contrary: our everyday life matters tremendously. Meditation is only a means of shaping it.

"To develop meditative thought" does not mean thinking *of* meditation, but developing thought *through* meditation.

THE PSYCHIC PROCESSES IN MEDITATION

THIS seems to be the most promising chapter, in that it holds out the hope that those who will not tread the weary path of experience may nevertheless, benefit from a detailed description of it.

When, now, I say that I shall not describe anything at all, then many will be put off and will despise me as a mystifier.

It is a sad but true fact that those who are aware of the existence of things beyond description, can usually find a way to them unaided, and that those who are not, will never believe that these things can *only* be experienced but never described.

"Be that as it may," they will retort, "but we'll manage all the same."

"Yes, but only just manage!"

Many try to describe the indescribable "roughly", and thus merely add to the confusion. However, if we have stayed the course of the first month of meditation without being overwhelmed by too many problems, our questions will be less urgent; and after two or three years we shall smile at those who ask the very questions we once asked ourselves.

Yet, in spite of all this, none of us will entirely refrain from trying to understand things, if only "roughly". We all draw conclusions from the most questionable of all syllogisms:

"Where there is nothing to think about, nothing can exist.
Here, however, something exists,
Therefore I should be able to think about it."

It cannot be stressed too much that here we are not dealing either with "something" or yet with "nothing".

Buddha said: "By analogy the true meaning of words may be made clear to reasonable people." Thus we shall try to describe the psychic process of meditation by means of a fairy-tale:

At the foot of a mountain called "Effort" and on whose

high peak there stood a shining castle—the castle of Truth—
there lived an old beggar by the name of Homosum.

Homosum did nothing but see to it that his stomach was
filled. For this he was beloved and esteemed as a valuable
member of society, for he always knew how to keep just on
the right side of hunger; and man does not judge with his
brain, but only with the stomach and the intestines.

The mountain was rightly called "Effort", for a great
effort was needed to climb it; and although Homosum and his
brothers would go to any lengths to keep alive, they were all
agreed that climbing the mountain was a sheer waste of energy.
After all, it could not matter less whether one inspected this
castle or not—it was no more than an uninteresting ruin. They
had seen quite enough of these, ruins were only for old wives
who could play cards and who couldn't take brandy.

"When I eat my fill, I know what I'm about; but when I
climb the mountain, I know nothing." This was the best-known
and the most common saying amongst the beggars.

One night Homosum had a terrible dream: he had to face
the judge of his clan. He awoke trembling, and brooded over
the fact that the axe could, in fact, fall at any minute, and that
he might become the victim of the law that those who are of
the mass are subject to the law of the mass. Only those who
climb above it may live as men.

"Climb! Climb!" he said to himself. And before the sun
has risen, he knew that there was only one way to climb above
the mass—the way despised by it: the way to the mountain of
Effort.

"If you must make an effort," his son said, scratching
himself lazily, "you might as well stay in the country and
earn your daily bread honestly. Here you know where you
are; here there is food and drink—what more do you want?
What can be more important than food and drink?"

"Are we born only to eat and drink?" Homosum asked
thoughtfully. His son laughed derisively:

"Brood away," he said, "you're sure to do great things!
Why don't you go and kill fat Possessus and bring us his
money? At least that would be productive. But to think why
we are born!" He scratched himself, grinned in a superior way,
shook his unwashed head and went out because he was hungry.

"He who has looked down from the mountain is cursed, for his eyes have been opened."

This was an ancient adage, once known to all but no longer understood by anybody. It was thought to be no more than an empty phrase. Indeed, even Homosum, who was now firm in his decision to climb the mountain of Effort, did not understand the meaning of these words.

He brooded for many hours on what might await him there, for "there had to be something"; and he painted tempting but unsatisfying pictures in his own phantasy. Yet he had a premonition that it would be something different—quite different from what people thought.

Once upon a time—so said the holy books—people had climbed it. And when they returned, they were called saints and law-makers. People no longer dared to call them "brothers", for only those are brothers who, too, are wretched, but those who returned were no longer so.

One day Homosum was ready: he had made the decision to lift himself above the mass, even if only by one step.

Firmly he approached the slope; the peak was enveloped in clouds. He climbed and climbed. Hours, days, weeks, years. However, every time he looked back to see how far he had come, he found to his consternation that he did not appear to have gone a single step forward; on the contrary, he thought he was nearer to the old world than ever before.

After a time, however, the old world became clearer, more transparent. The farther he climbed, the more could be seen through the walls of the houses, through the hearts and the cares of men, and the more did he lose his desire to escape from his world. And yet, in spiritual certainty, he climbed higher and higher, borne by the force of the dawning knowledge, which became stronger with every step, that it was neither time nor desire which brought him nearer to his goal, but only the very steps of this ascent. Near though he remained to his world, he yet became free of its suffering. But when he spoke of this, nobody understood him.

He called: "Follow me on to the mountain! You will find greater peace, you will be able to see through your cares as if they were glass, your world will become greater, more beautiful and more holy!"

But they only laughed at him, and this laughter was like the screeching of monkeys. The few who did not laugh asked: "Explain your words! What do you mean by them?"

"Just come!" he called till he was out of breath, "come and see for yourself!"

"What, dear friend, do you want us to see that we cannot see from here?" they replied politely and reasonably, "if you can see more things than we do, very well, we shall come, for we have always been very interested in magic with which to harm our enemies; but you, you say yourself that you can see no more than we do. Why go to the trouble of climbing?"

The higher he climbed the more solitary Homosum became, but the more solitary he became, the happier he was. For this solitude was not loneliness, it was an inner harmony, and he felt all distractions to be a mere burden.

"There is no loneliness," he called down, "if one is satisfied with oneself!" And again they laughed:

"Poor devil, he is out of his mind!" And the more he called to them, the more they ran home, for they were ashamed to have been his friend.

Even that did not hurt him any more, for he saw their hearts, saw whether they were made of gold, silver or pebble-stones; and when he looked into their eyes, it was as if he looked into a book; and the only surprise was that he had not seen before what now appeared so simple and clear.

"It's all so natural," he thought, "so childishly natural! What a world!"

Years passed. He no longer climbed with great effort—he rose by his inner forces. He had forgotten his one-time longing for the peak.

Now he was infinitely happy, infinitely peaceful, yet still he could see no more than those, who slowly overtaken by embarrassed silence, looked at him with shy eyes, and suddenly raised their hands like little children wanting to go home and afraid.

One day he looked and realized that the mountain was endless. He kept silent, for how could he tell those longing for a goal, "There is no goal that you can see with your eyes."

"Have you reached the castle of Truth?" he was asked.

The castle of Truth! That's what they call the goal. He

remembered. And suddenly he realized that the mountain was no mountain at all, but a carpet of flowers in a stately hall.

"But where is the mountain?" he asked himself in surprise, and at that moment he knew that the mountain was his own body, his own desire, his own suffering; and that he and his brothers had always been living in the castle of Truth. Now he knew: daily—throughout their whole miserable lives—they had made a mountain from heaps of sand and stone, the better to hide the castle of truth.

"We must climb the mountain," he said, "not for the peak's sake, but in order to raise ourselves. We must overcome desire, not in order to reach our goal but to attain greater peace."

He saw that he had been blind and that there were no more questions at all.

Although he stood amidst his brethren, he could see through them like crystal, through all that they feared or worshipped. He saw how their hearts beat, how their brains worked, how the blood circulated, how they gazed at the ground when they spoke of the stars, how they fell on their knees before pictures, and how they fled in confusion whenever a glimmer from the castle of Truth penetrated their confused brooding.

They had learned to long for distant goals, and they looked at the peak with tears of hope in their tired eyes.

"Climb!" he said. "Begin to climb!"

"Why?" they asked. "We love our longing. One day we'll reach it."

"But it is in you and around you!"

"No," they said with unshakable conviction, "it is high as the heavens. Haven't you climbed it yourself? Why did you do it, and now you say that Truth is amongst us?"

Homosum sighed for he knew that his words were empty:

"In order to find Truth by looking back. Truth always lies just there where we wish to escape. We must climb high above the mountain of our suffering and of our blindness, and everything that we have looked for with such longing, will lie before us."

AN OUTLINE OF THE COURSE OF MEDITATION

THOSE who have fully understood the previous chapter may now expect satisfaction from meditation, and will approach it with patient faith and with a minimum of scepticism and prejudice. Those, on the other hand, who are sceptical rather than convinced and nevertheless tackle the subject practically, expect a miracle, a magical result. To enter into battle without believing in victory is either suicide or a game of chance. Here it would mean a waste of time.

On the other hand, it would be just as bad to pretend to be convinced by the evidence of others, and without any positive personal experiences, for this would be believing without seeing.

Buddha said to his pupils:

"You must not simply believe what I say, you must discover the truth *for yourselves*. I only show you the path. Yet you should not follow it merely because *I* have recommended it, but only because you have recognized it as the true path in your deepest soul."

It is not sufficient merely to believe in a supposed truth, it must be experienced in one's deepest self; one must truly possess what one believes. There is a beautiful story to illustrate the theory and practice of true inner conviction:

A pious country parson was invited for a drive by his nephew who was visiting him. Unlike his reverend uncle, the young man loved speed and therefore stepped on the accelerator so hard that the good parson sweated blood. He sat huddled in the corner of his seat and muttered continuously:

"Everything is in the hands of the Lord. Nothing can happen to His children if it does not please Him. We can do nothing if the Lord does not will it. It behoves us to be resigned to His decisions, for His hand is held protectively over good and evil," and so on. Till he could not contain himself any longer and shouted at his nephew:

"I can't stand it any longer! Either you slow down at once or I get out! You are going to kill the two of us!"

This little story is not meant to caricature the parson's lack of faith in God, but to show that it is only correct and natural to condemn the shirking of decisions as mental and spiritual laziness and as cowardice. We should be very careful and sceptical when judging so-called piousness, for very often it is no more than a cloak for inability, indecisiveness or lack of a sense of responsibility. Indeed, it is a perversion to behave towards current difficulties like a rabbit before a snake, and to make religious humility an excuse for our cowardice. It is easy to blame some higher power for our misfortunes, particularly since our laziness of thought rebels against inner activity. As the Japanese adage has it:

"As long as I stand on the bridge, the river is still and the bridge flows."

We *know* that the sun stands still and that the earth moves, but our daily *experience* is quite the opposite. We observe a change and believing that we are constant, we logically conclude that it is *God* who creates, sends, knows, wills, threatens and rewards.

Those who decide to discover true religion in themselves will be able to solve this problem without profaning or denigrating any of the things which have always been held in reverence.

And, after all, why should this happen?

When deeper understanding makes everything more profound, when even a fish becomes more significant, how could what is humanity's highest good suddenly become profaner, more insignificant through a clearer and deeper conviction, through the unclouded contemplation of our own depth? On the contrary: only if we lift ourselves from blind familiarity and prejudice into active faith will our deepest natural conviction become a source of the highest and purest certainty.

We *know* that we are restless and wish to overcome this physical restlessness. It is for this reason that without philosophizing about it, we train to lie still, not to force matters, but merely to become more peaceful, to gain greater self-mastery. We *know* that we are the victims of a mad whirlwind of thought, that hitherto we had no other way to "enlightenment" than

J

the uncertain feeling (our so-called "belief") that the true source of our eternal forces lay beyond thought. Now we begin to collect our thoughts, to concentrate, to free ourselves slowly from the curse of time, to see clearly what previously was vaguely suspected.

When we have reached this point, then we have reached a level from which we can see farther and better.

Now we *know* that we are not simply accepting the statements of others, but have such an indescribable feeling of certainty, springing from our own pure and deep experience, that we are filled with a great vision. We no longer follow anything that is uncertain, but experience our inner soul as an integral part of religion. We do so more and more, from day to day. What is once experienced can never be lost.

It is with this infinitely strong, and therefore infinitely happy assurance which bathes our entire lives in a clear light, that we enter our meditation chamber and for some hours of meditation we look at ourselves closely.

The difficulties and the achievements cited here are naturally only *one* combination chosen at random from an infinite number of possibilities. Everybody will experience them in a different order, but there is hardly one who will escape them entirely. One will experience one obstacle, another a different one. One will overcome it more quickly, another more slowly; but everyone will have to come to terms with it sooner or later. Yet nobody need fear that *his* difficulties are especially great. There are *no* difficulties which cannot be overcome, it is only a question of time and patience. Once mastered, they will never return.

It will be shown that what prevented meditation was, in fact, precisely what made life itself so impossible. For everything which disturbs our lives also disturbs meditation; and everything which helps meditation, also helps our tranquillity and our success in daily life. Meditation is never for a single moment a strange world of its own.

Now we have sat down on our carefully prepared cushion, do not feel the slightest pressure of a belt, or collar, etc., are as much at ease as possible, and there is no danger that after five minutes we will find to our irritation that we are extremely uncomfortable. A deep breath, similar to the one at night when we pull the covers over our ears, indicates that we are content within, and thus meditation begins. This breath is a physical token of the fact that we are free of desire, if only for the moment.

If, perchance, we have decided to shorten the period of meditation of that day by just a little because we are so pressed for time, we must nevertheless, try not to rush through it. For after all, no poet will say, "Today I must write three poems, but I must write them quickly as I have to call at the Ministry of Finance." He will write only one poem but he will do it well. He will do less, but do it correctly.

Further, we must never say:

"I must be careful of the time, for when I am deeply immersed I may not notice that it is getting too late."

We can forget such or similar fears completely, for never yet has it happened that anybody has missed anything of great importance through meditation.

However, this has happened very often when one is *not* concentrated. It is a strange but incontestable fact that we can concentrate on any object whatsoever and that we are, nevertheless on time, if what we are afraid of missing is really important.

This is proof of the careful guard kept by the subconscious and is known to us by the strange phenomenon of punctual waking.

We must say to ourselves: the world has ceased to exist for the moment. Outside these four walls there is a desert which does not interest me in the least.

But, note well, do not *force* yourself to think of anything definite, for all those thoughts with a rebellious need for freedom would be up in arms. True, they must be disciplined to respond to our command, but it is easier to tame a fly than one's own thoughts.

To master them we not only require patience but a great deal of diplomacy. Time after time we must let them run their courses patiently and amicably, in order, time after time, to pull them by the lead with a "come, come!" At the start this seems hopeless, but it is merely difficult.

"Just as difficult, or perhaps even more so, is it to shut out thought altogether. In the beginning it will not be possible for more than about five seconds; but after a year, for more than a minute. The difficulty of this exercise lies in the fact that one doesn't notice "thoughts creeping back", but suddenly *remembers*, while one has long been brooding about something, that actually one didn't want to think of anything at all. If, for a short time we had no thoughts *at all*, then not even the thought, "Don't think of anything," could have arisen.

But back to the practical exercise!

Throughout the first week we want to do no more than become accustomed to the atmosphere of our meditation chamber.

We want to become very familiar with our environment and therefore, look with great care and interest at everything around us. For at least two weeks and for at least ten minutes and not longer than twenty or thirty minutes at a time.

Here we do not even want the following prejudice to arise:

"Dash it, there is nothing to see on the walls; I don't have to look at them!"

Nothing is uninteresting, only prejudice. *Whether* the wall is interesting or not, can only be determined after at least one week.

And should we think: "I can do it much more quickly," then even a week might be inadequate. After all, there is nothing for us to expect or to miss, we must only absorb— even with our eyes and with the surface of the skin. This sucking in of the atmosphere may sometimes (and not slowly, but very suddenly) become boring. This is an important sign, but unfortunately not a positive one, for it simply means that other distracting thoughts are rather unfairly demanding admission by deluding us that they are more important than quiet attention. But still, we wish to be conciliatory and not to fight one prejudice with another. We leave our observation, open the door to the thoughts, and let them come.

One thing, however, we must remember: attention. Only now we pay it to the thoughts rushing into our head.

We investigate *what* thought is demanding admission and we try to determine *why* it demands admission; we think about the sudden thought, or better, we make it an object of meditation.

This we shall only be able to do for a little while, for another thought will be asking admission and this too, we observe carefully, until after a few minutes we again take the initiative and return to our starting-point.

We allow this to happen a number of times, and then with just as deep a breath as at the beginning, we end the meditàtive exercise.

This—as we said before—will continue for a few weeks.

Only when we get the pleasant feeling that this absolutely immobile way of sitting is somehow extremely soothing and restful, does our attentive attitude change, and we do nothing but enjoy the peace, just as we enjoy the first few minutes in a comfortable chair after a tiring day. In that case also, we merely think:

How very peaceful and nice it is! What a great pleasure!

As soon as active thinking begins anew, peace has gone. Therefore, we must try to remain as free of thought as possible, even if at the start we shall only succeed for a very short time.

Oddly, the first thought which enters our apparently empty consciousness is the thought of breathing, for we suddenly "notice" that we are breathing.

This thought we may gladly welcome and we may consciously observe the "pump of life", but with this friendly hint to our breath:

"Please don't be disturbed, but carry on as you usually do!"

Well, it won't listen, and—just like a pupil under the eyes of his teacher—it will become far more active, but only until it gets used to the observer.

Then, however, we may discover some very interesting things, for instance, that during very great concentration breath may stop altogether for quite a long time. I myself, became aware of this quite by accident:

I had the misfortune to be living in a very unhealthy part of India and, during the rainy season especially, I suffered from some unpleasant complaints. One night of terrible breathing pains, in particular, I shall never forget.

It was only concentration which helped me to bear these pains, for throughout the night I had to lie absolutely still, and to stand the pain at all, I had to breathe as little as possible. The next day the doctor came. He listened to my heart and lungs, and I was so withdrawn both because of my pain-relieving concentration and physical weakness that I was only brought back to myself by his question: "How do you do it? I have been listening to your lungs for the last five minutes without your having taken a single breath all this time."

I myself hadn't noticed anything, for as soon as my attention was brought back, breathing proceeded in its usual rhythm; and my conscious attempts to arrest it only produced that well-known unpleasant feeling of suffocation, and increased my already great pain.

Just as I only became aware of this phenomenon indirectly, so will nobody else be able to make this strange discovery consciously, for after all, breathing is only a *means* in the service of concentration and meditation, never an aim in itself.

The endeavour to control breathing consciously is simply the result of misunderstanding the purpose of these exercises, and only proves that we are trying to develop supernatural faculties. This, however, we should and may never do. These faculties will arise quite naturally, and the mature consciousness and modesty of those who have understood the deeper meaning of meditation will take them very seriously, but never use them sensationally.

As soon as the mind has become accustomed to independent breathing observation, we begin that series of exercises described in the chapter called "The Observation of Breathing".

It is advisable to keep the eyes slightly, but never too tightly, closed so that the eyes muscles are not tensed.

The position of the eyes when the lids are closed is not exactly the same as in sleep. It is as if we looked at an object about eight inches distant, directly in front of us, i.e. the eyes are turned slightly inwards.

This prevents both our falling asleep and that disturbing tension which arises when, following the suggestions of Hatha Yoga, we look at the tip of our nose. Hatha Yoga does this for a special reason which need not be discussed here.

During the exercise we breathe through the nose. The mouth is closed, and the entire tongue lies close to the lower teeth. In other words: the mouth is *very slightly* tensed. This is done because no concentrated thinking is possible at all if all the muscles of speech are *completely* relaxed.

On the other hand it is important to see that the rest of the body is relaxed, and we do so during those all too frequent intervals of concentration when we give free rein to our straying thoughts. This applies particularly to the parts around the eyes, the forehead and the root of the nose.

In this exercise, too, we may become bored, and we must treat this boredom just as we did in the previous exercise.

Only when we are sure that we can spend at least five minutes on one exercise without being distracted, may we think of entering into meditation beyond concentration. Here, too, there is no abrupt transition, but only a natural sliding.

Through absolute concentration, thought has become as peaceful as a calm sea. Into this sea we now drop the object of meditation, as if it were a stone.

It is not a case of giving our thoughts free rein apart from directing them to a certain object: it is not active thought-*work* which must be done now, but what happens is that consciousness—now clear as the sea—no longer rests in itself, but on a picture or a concept (*cf.*, objects of meditation). There is no longer a "thinking about", but only "pictures or concepts *in* thought".

The only thing that has been discarded is prejudice. What remains is a mirror of pure consciousness.

However, before we reach this, many years may have passed. Time after time, active thought will want to go its own way; and time after time, we shall have to give in until our quiet will proves itself the stronger, the victor. Then the door to everything is open, for then we are free from all deception. Not everybody will be able to reach this point, for the path is long—for many longer than life itself.

But many will be able to experience the goal for seconds, as some reward for their tenacity. Those who have experienced these seconds of pure contemplation will know that no effort has been too great, that they have found a treasure whose value will be appreciated most when their need is greatest.

Meditation is as manifold as life itself.

Today—obvious failure, which will afterwards prove to have benefited us; tomorrow—success which will only lead to new difficulties, but never a straight course to success. Life, however, is such that in spite of all failure or lack of success, we shall one day nevertheless be mature and experienced men. The same applies to meditation which, while requiring a constant vigilance against confusion of thought for many years, nevertheless elevates us in the course of our endeavours.

There will be days (always few and far between), on which we shall be able to say with joy and with victorious pride:

"Well now, finally I have made it! Now I can do it!"

Yet the next day things are worse than they have ever been before; and it may only too easily happen that we conclude that the whole of meditation is nonsense, although only yesterday we were ready to stake our lives on it.

The isolated days of apparent success are the so-called rewards which are worthless in themselves, and are no more than small momentary incentives. They are like the sweets which the child is given when it is required to go to school; at first it only goes because of the sweets, and then it learns; not through those sweets, but with the psychological aid of these sweets, for they give him pleasure, and we need a little pleasure now and then to spur us on.

On the next day, however, we must account for our pleasure, and the account—as most of them—is usually unpleasant. At first we think we are thrown back, and in a way we really are; for the joyful expectation of equal success in the future is precisely what we had overcome, and is only too ready to re-emerge to create the well-known obstacle anew.

It will take us a few days to forget this "success" of the one isolated day, and for the path of systematic development to run quite peacefully again.

Indeed, out of a clear sky days will appear in which self-recollection will be almost impossible, and on which we believe that we have "done something wrong", because we "can't make progress".

Those who, because of this, abandon meditation, have not succumbed to the difficulties of meditation, but to their own short-comings. For in meditation there are no natural obstacles. These are only found in man himself.

Some short-comings, however, must not be suppressed, they must be lived out, they must—like the snowman in the sun—thaw away to nothing without our impatient assistance.

TOTAL MEDITATION

From all the above we may conclude that the whole of meditation consists of overlapping stages. Although they are different, each stage contains the germ of the one above it. Throughout, there is a constant liberation from extra-conscious elements, until there remains only consciousness alone, but not its activity. Consciousness is *directed*, but no longer *active*. This can be expressed as follows:

Those active components which lie between the soul and consciousness, such as our experiences (picture and concept), our judgments (positive or negative), our active will (for or against), in short, everything which produces decisions based on experience, everything guided by feeling and supported by the will, becomes passive and disengaged. Because of this, a straight and unobstructed path leads directly from consciousness to the soul, a path which knows no illusions but only the immediate and absolute truth.

Under these circumstances time itself ceases, because there is no longer any process, nothing *becomes*, everything *is*.

This is the immediate experience of eternity!

Everything which normally does not belong to consciousness (or belongs to it only by its manifestations) can now be experienced immediately, i.e. nct in its picture, but in *itself*.

The above, however, is not a very good explanation since the very word "itself" is completely misleading, and assumes a "something", in other words, a material concept, and this is not what we mean.

Here now in this first step of timeless experiences, we recognize absolute space. Not space as the unit of volume, not *a* space, but infinite, unexpanding space.

This is the first step of total meditation which can only be reached after the attainment of that absolute concentration which is always associated with the highest degree of meditation.

The next step is potentially contained in the previous one,

but now it takes the form of *pure enlightenment* without any pictorial concepts, for these we have long discarded.

Now we shall discover a polarity between the seer (absolute consciousness) and the seen (the eternal), both of which are inseparably bound to each other just like plus and minus, mountain and valley, like the two halves of a circle. Here we have infinite consciousness experiencing absolute space.

Here, too, neither pictures nor concepts are formed, nothing in fact which we can include in our store of experience.

The best illustration of how little our concepts can describe these processes is given by the famous question of Zen Buddhism:

"If I clap my hands, which is the sound of the right hand?"

The third step is made up of the recognition of the result of this polarity between space and consciousness, its unreality, its emptiness, its unity. This was called Unio Mystica by Christian mystics when speaking of the same process. Those who, in meditation, have known a measure of deep inner experience themselves, and who read the words of Master Eckhart or of Jacob Böhme, will see their own experiences confirmed there. What the essential difference is we shall discuss when we deal with Christian Mystics.

We have only been able to give a rough description of the psychological processes, because of the paucity of language. The last, the highest, the fourth step, however, cannot even be described roughly, for there are no comparisons to indicate it at all. We have no words to describe what lies behind the core of all unity. This much is certain—it is the highest goal of all religion and of all faiths.

Perhaps the name given to it by Christian Mystics is the best—it is "a mystical death".

We do not want to delay the reader with fruitless speculations, for it is better to remain factual for a hundred pages than to rave for even one page over a goal to which we do not know the way.

Nevertheless, the opinion prevalent even in the East, that total meditation cannot be attained by anyone today is quite baseless.

Everyone can experience it, if only for one happy fraction of a single moment. And if as wise old men, having nurtured each hour of meditation with infinite patience, we had experienced but this one fleeting moment, our life-long labours would not have been in vain. This moment, this fraction of eternal enlightenment, will have been lifted clear out of time, will become an eternity and be the very purpose of all our existence.

Thus we have reached the end. Have we really done so? No, for we haven't even begun. For as long as we have not discarded everything meant by the words "saying" and "understanding", and as long as we have not entered that great strange gate through which we have to pass naked as at birth or in death—the gate of experience—so long has our true life not even begun. For life does not want to be "said" or "understood": life will and must be lived. As is now and ever has been, so it will be forever more. Ever since we first said "I" we have been afraid of the great Judge. We seek Him with our eyes although we have long known Him in our hearts; for while our eyes are blind, our hearts have a thousand eyes; and the greater the darkness, the clearer can the heart see the path.

We always seek enlightenment, but we do not recognize it because we are confused, and the beat of our heart is too soft.

We coin words and names which are as empty as space, as the space in which they echo. "Faith," we say, and believe in the word and the name; but we do not know anything about "Faith" itself. Thus a mere *word* can become our greatest barrier to thought, if we do not know the path, if we do not trust our hearts, if we wish to delude ourselves about certainties where none are to be found, if we speak of a faith as a mere aimless, vague concept, guilt-laden, and revelling in self-reproach.

No, it is not true that belief is the greatest of our treasures. We can do more than merely form words. We also have the power of experiencing *without words* that absolute certainty which is above all belief and more silent than death, if the eyes of the heart remain closed. Who will cast the first stone at us when, with desperate lies, we wish to flee from ourselves; when our blindness has robbed us of the only, the ultimate and the holiest strength, wherewith to bear the truth of life?

We turn our backs to the Sun, and we are satisfied to see our world reflected in its rays.

But where there is light there must be shadows. We wander about the world seeking the light, when all we have to do to partake of it, is to turn round and to leave the shadows behind us.

Then at last we may shut our own eyes, for the eyes of the heart will recognize the light a thousand times more clearly. Then life will become a thousand times richer, for the burden will have been lifted from our shoulders; nothing can frighten us any more—nothing is mightier than the radiance and the immortal happiness of truth.

Our path does not end where we thought we were lost. It ends when we return home after all our roaming, and we have nothing more to lose, where there is no end because the uncertainty of the beginning, the dark quest of "whither?" has become the happy "at last!"

We know that there is a home for each one of us if only we do not allow our false "beliefs" to fritter our lives away. We have but to ask and we shall be answered. We have but to knock, and it will be opened unto us. Often we shall have to knock till our hands are raw, and despair of those who pointed the thorny path to the gate.

Until one day we shall suddenly understand the deep wisdom of these very great words written above the gate in glowing letters:

"KNOW THYSELF!"

APPENDICES

MEDITATION IN JAPANESE ZEN-BUDDHISM

ZEN is the name of the leading Buddhist sect in Japan which has existed since the twelfth century. The Japanese word "Zen" is derived from the Chinese word "Ch'an", and this in turn comes from the Sanskrit. There it is called Dhyana. The meaning of this word in all three languages is: meditation.

Everything that we find so strange in Japanese culture is inseparably bound up with the meditative character of Zen-Buddhism, and from it there arise the mysterious cults: the liberating beauty of "home ritual"[1] the festive thoughtfulness of the "tea ritual" (cha-no-yu)[2], the fabulous arts of the "flower ritual", of water-colours, of poetry, or archery, and even of fencing; in short, from ju-jutsu to philosophy—everything has its origin in the spirit of Zen.

What is Zen? Meditation, certainly, but much more than that. Immeasurable potentialities are hidden in this modest source. It is the birth of natural wisdom and of natural beauty. It is so simple and so natural, that our confused senses cannot believe it, look for something "behind" it, go around in circles and become confused. We despair because we have run past the aim for so long, because we constantly believe "we ought to be able to think it all out". The Zen-Master, however, smiles and with his smile destroys everything that thinking, brooding, calculation, proofs, logic and reason have carefully constructed.

Zen cannot be described, it can only be experienced. But just as it is difficult to describe it, so is it easy to experience Zen. Only, experience must be freed from the burden of thought. Those who can distinguish between *thoughtlessness* and *freedom from thought*, have not far to go to find Zen.

It is just the same here as with everything else in life: the best way is always the most natural way, for it is the shortest;

[1] If we compare the simplicity of our meditation chamber with that of the Japanese living-room, we shall find a striking resemblance.
[2] Here, again, but on a higher level, there applies what we said about the meditation of eating. For the "tea ritual" after all, is no cult in the usual ritual sense, but a purely meditative process.

but—call it faith, Karma, or curse—we always prefer the path of tortuous thought: the logical "thoughtful" and calculated way, as if life itself were logical or calculable.

Zen asks neither for logic nor for reason, but only for facts, so naked that to us who are so fettered with logic, they appear completely incomprehensible.

There is little sense in trying to explain the subtle wisdom of Zen with mere words. Many good books have been written on it without succeeding in their attempts to explain theoretically, what in experience, has proven to be so simple and clear. It cannot be done, and we shall not try it here.

However, I should like to relate two little stories—one historical and one which happened to me—which serve to show that any word of explanation is left miles behind by experience itself; how it only affects our thoughts, while true experience goes empty-handed. And yet the simplest, if indefinable way, is experience itself!

A young monk approached a Master of Zen and asked: "What is Buddhism?"

The Master kept silent, and the young man repeated his question, since he thought that the Master had not heard him.

The Master simply took a cup and gracefully dropped it to the ground where it broke. Then did the young man see the light of wisdom.

In order to understand the significance of this story, we *must* have experienced it. After reflecting on it we might well find beautiful and suitable explanations for the action of the Master, but this is not the point at all for the Master did not want to explain anything.

Only because he understood the wisdom of the Master *immediately*, without using the by-path of logical thought (he had no time for this), did he become enlightened. For enlightenment is not intellectual conviction (that would be philosophy), but immediate experience.

Perhaps my own experience may serve the purpose even better, because it moves on the same level, and it gave me a very clear understanding of the experience involved:

I have forgotten with whom I was having this discussion. I only know that it was somewhere in Asia, and that the discussion was about some subtle problem of Buddhism.

We were both deep in discussion, and I had to be most alert, since a discussion of philosophy and metaphysics in a foreign tongue requires the fullest activity of the mind, even if one should have mastered the subject.

It was obvious that my whole thought machine was active but that the realm of experience was completely dormant, as is customary in intellectual discussions.

Whether it was to make some point, or whether it was for no purpose at all (even this I have forgotten), in any case, unexpectedly and very suddenly, and as far as I was concerned, quite irrelevantly, the other clapped his hands.

In that instant the unbridgeable gulf between thought and experience became so plastically clear to me as never before. For some seconds I was beyond all thought and felt the radiance of pure enlightenment. I know that had this hand-clapping been logical or intellectually bound up with my thoughts, it would have passed me by just as the words did. Only because it was completely outside the closed circle of the intellect did it, like an arrow, hit the very centre of another sphere which beyond all logic lies in pure experience, and thus on a higher, purer and more enlightened level. Here words are no longer needed to convince, here the force of conviction, due to pure unanalysable experience, leads to the highest enlightenment. This is Zen.

Here thought is not only superfluous, but is an obstacle to pure experience, that shock-wave which plumbs the spiritual depths so quickly that no inhibiting thought can obstruct it. It is a complete process of meditation in the fraction of one single second. And this is more than enough, for as we saw in the previous chapter, we do not need long periods to recognize truth which is the soul itself, it is only pictures and concepts which require time and space. Immediate inner perception takes place on a different level.

It is the same level from which Buddha could survey all his previous existences within the space of one moment; it is the level from which Mozart experienced a whole concert in the fraction of a second, but to write it down took many weeks.

It is, however, also that level which, from the moment of the great divide, from that immeasurably short instant of death onwards, enters as "eternity" into our last ray of consciousness: as "eternal damnation" or as "eternal salvation".

But this is not "eternal" in the sense of being "endless", but in the sense of being "beyond all time". And here, too, it is our own guilt or merit which decides whether we flee from the judge who, beyond conscious understanding, sentences us with the tremendous force of an impenetrable dream. We grasp that door which attracts us most strongly, which corresponds best to our natural characteristics acquired during our long unreflecting lives. For thought does not exist, only timeless and impulsive, i.e. instinctive action. Thus we believe that we can escape our guilt and all the fears of hell, and for that very reason we take them into our new existence. Here, if we can, we hold everyone responsible for this apparently unjust burden but ourselves.

Our "fate" is our own work and it is also our judge. It follows us farther than thought.

What follows death is not reward or punishment, it is that half of the great scale which, while it rests in darkness, rises and falls according to whether we load or free that half which is our life. What a clear and simple law!

The timeless ray of enlightenment, however, allows us to look into the dark. And those who dare look beyond the confining walls of prejudice and thought, directly into immediate experience, are beyond the riddle of past and future.

The life and training of Zen monks serve this purpose. Nothing is farther from them than mystical and secret doctrines. Zen is an immediate union with all that goes to make up daily life.

These monks grow their own food, busily tilling their own land, for physical labour is healthy and near to life. Just as is Zen.

Life in the Zen monastery begins long before the sun rises. Physical and spiritual labour is wisely balanced. No more is spoken than is absolutely necessary, and all meals are taken communally and in silence.

Every monk has been given a problem—a *koan*—by the Master, with which to occupy his inner self for days, weeks, yes sometimes even for years, until one day, through the path of inner contemplation, he arrives at the enlightening answers (*satori*).

May I be permitted to refer to a little book which, as no other, gives an idea of the way and the method of Zen. The author, a German sage, who for many years was a lecturer at Tokio University, devoted himself to the practical study of

Zen, and wrote a short and yet complete, even dramatic, survey of the course of his education. Here no crank speaks, but a serious, thorough, open-hearted scientist.[1]

Let us listen to his description of the archery of his Master (pages 71-72):

I sat opposite him on a cushion. He passed me a cup of tea, but did not speak. We sat thus for a long time. We could hear nothing but the singing of the kettle of boiling water. Finally, the Master rose and beckoned me to follow him. The gymnasium was brightly illuminated. The Master told me to put a mosquito candle, long and thin like a knitting-needle, in front of the target, but not to switch on the light over it. It was so dark that I could not even see the contours of the target, and if the tiny spark of the mosquito candle had not given it away, I might have suspected the position of the target, but I could not have made it out. The Master "danced" the ceremony. His first arrow was shot from radiant brightness into deep night. By the sound I could hear that he had hit the target. The second arrow too, was well-aimed. When I switched on the light over the target, I discovered to my astonishment that the first arrow had hit the bull's-eye, while the second had splintered the first one and had cut its shaft open before boring into the bull's-eye next to it. I did not dare to pull the arrows out one by one, but I returned them both together with the target. The Master looked at them carefully.

"The first hit may not appear a great feat to you," he said, "since you will say that I have been so familiar with the position of the target for decades, that it should not have been too difficult to hit it even in the dark. Be that as it may, I do not wish to change your mind. What do you think of the second arrow hitting the first? I for one know that it was not 'I' who should be given credit for this shot. 'It' simply shot, 'it' hit. Let us bow to the aim as if it were the Buddha!"

What was it again that we said of the hand-clapping? Had the arrow been guided by logical thought, had it been aimed, thought would have led it elsewhere. Here, however, the arrow hit the very centre of the soul. Let us bow down before the aim, as if it were the Buddha!

[1] Eugen Herrigel: *Zen in der Kunst des Bogenschiessens* (Zen in the Art of Archery), C. Weller, Konstanz, 1948.

K

MEDITATION IN THE WONDERLAND OF TIBET

CIVILIZATION is an enemy of spiritual development, for it serves the satisfaction of material needs alone. Civilization makes life pleasant, i.e. it makes it easy for man to forget his inner responsibilities. But regrettable though it might be, it is, nevertheless, a quite natural striving of humanity to choose the most pleasant way of life, and to forget all the unpleasantness caused by our own inadequacy. Thus it has come about that a people is judged by its civilization rather than by its culture which, though it has more modest manifestations, makes far greater demands. Whereas culture is of the heart, civilization is no more than a veneer. There are only a few who know that Tibet, the secret country behind the folds of the Himalayas, is one of the most cultured countries on earth. All we do know is that it is one of the poorest in civilization, for there are no trains, no cars, no cinema, indeed, not even a newspaper.[1]

The traveller is strangely touched by the fact that in even the most primitive villages, he will find temples in which are stored works of art of breath-taking beauty. These are by no means only works of times long past, but here the ancient is harmoniously coupled with the modern. The popular art of Tibet today, just as a thousand years ago, is of a surprisingly high standard.

Tibet is a purely Buddhistic country; and the religious philosophy of its people is—even with their complete lack of civilization—of a spiritual and mental depth, and at the same time of so admirable a nearness to life, that we may call this people one of the most spiritual peoples on earth.

No other people has so comprehensive a philosophical literature, and no other lives in so immediate a unity with the philosophy of its religion.

All the elements that went into it—from Mongolia in the north, from China in the east, from Nepal and India in the

---

[1] The only newspaper appearing in the Tibetan language is printed in India.

south, from the old Orient and Europe itself in the west—were absorbed intelligently and with inner self-certainty. Nothing new was added to the old, before it was understood, only then was it absorbed and gracefully incorporated, and thus enriched the whole. It was no foreign body such as we find in Gandhara art, or in the innumerable independent stylistic elements of Indian art of the Middle Ages—but an affirmation of its own inner diversity: the present.

The basis for all this creative independence is found in the certainty and absolute clarity of their philosophy, in the knowledge of what is essential, in their absolutely clear self-recognition, and in their recognition of the truly religious elements of life which are ever alive in their profoundest depths, in short, in their meditative results.

The intuitive perception of the Fathers, the wisdom of the holy books of religion, indeed, all religions observed today, find their counterparts even *now* amongst the holy men of Tibet; if only in rare cases.

These great sages who live in the caves of the Himalayas far from all human habitation, who develop their natural faculties in years—and even decades—of hard schooling, are beyond all limitation, for their wisdom far transcends the ridiculous business of the world.

These men are rightly an example for every religious Tibetan, who (today as ever) does not judge the merit and the venerability of a man by his possessions, his rank, or his age, but by the measure of his wisdom alone, be he a beggar, or even—strangest of all possibilities—a stranger, a European.

Everywhere in Tibet around the large monasteries there are small, empty single-storey houses. They do not belong to anyone because they belong to everyone—they are "houses of meditation". Whoever—villager, lama, stranger or abbot—wishes to retire here for a certain time to meditate without disturbance, will be richly and gladly supplied with food by the population, and can be certain of everyone's protection and help.

Generally people retire for three months. Some do it for years, and there have been cases where pious lamas allowed themselves to be immured for the rest of their lives. Only when the food placed into a hole in the wall, is found untouched, are the wall and door broken down so that the dead lama, who has now become a saint, may be honourably buried.

This year-long or life-long solitude is not infrequently carried out in complete darkness.

We do not wish to judge or to criticize; for in order to understand these things we must at least have taken a small step in the same direction.

This, however, is certain: to these men, lifelong "darkness" means more than reading an entire library does to us. I have frequently made their acquaintance, and without exception I was always gripped to the very core of my being by the power of the personality of these saints.

We need no longer ask: "How can they stand their year-long solitude, and what is more, in complete darkness? How is it that they do not go mad?"

After all our discussion we should know that where thought and pictures and concepts have been superseded, there exists neither time nor loneliness, indeed, neither light nor darkness. Here there is nothing we can imagine and also nothing which we cannot imagine.

We have no idea as yet, of what a human being can achieve, who has lived in complete seclusion for decades. There are many credible reports about the miraculous powers of these mysterious people.

It has been proved that, in a state of total meditation, they are capable of running for hundreds of kilometres without stopping, and at so great a speed that even a rider on horseback cannot follow them. They have the power of appearing at several places at the same time, and they can sit naked on the ice during a polar Tibetan winter, and while remaining motionless for days and nights, even melt the snow around them. By the simple power of thought they can send messages to distant friends, can read the thoughts of others as a book, and can immediately heal wounds of even the greatest severity. Our imagination is quite inadequate to picture their powers.

But all these abilities are not goals of meditative development; they are accompanying symptoms which are mistaken for the actual goal by only a very few adepts.

The Tibetan keeps his miraculous powers a closely guarded secret. Even more closely does he guard the true inner goal that he has attained, for it is a fact which cannot be stressed too often:

We may discuss meditation as such without harm; but if we give away a part of our *own* experiences and successes, then they are lost. It is unnecessary to add that this is not an occult, but a psychological fact. It is not very surprising that the "modern city dweller" is sceptical of this highest meditative achievement, and simply rejects it as a fairy-tale since "such things are quite impossible".

However, there is no need for you to believe in it. Indeed, if you did, and strove with all your might towards it, you would only be miserably disappointed. This is a good thing, for to do so is to play with your life.

The path of meditation of the Tibetan Yoga is the direct path, i.e. the path which spiritually surmounts all obstacles on the way. No other way of meditation is nearly as successful, but the slightest wrong step may lead to madness or death.[1] We can and may only follow it under the expert guidance of a teacher (a Guru), and it could not be otherwise, since the methods are kept a careful secret, and are only transmitted orally from teacher to pupil. What we possess in written directions is incomplete, veiled and only very partially comprehensible. Even if the inquisitive should manage to enter the "Land of the Gods" with a stolen text, and if he were to search for a Guru—he would never find him until he has the requisite inner maturity. If he has not, he may live for years in the house of a master of meditation, without even suspecting who is his host.

If he is mature, however, he will find him, even without looking for him. For it is the strangest and most beautiful of all laws of spiritual development:

The master is there when the time is ripe.

Strangely enough, the dangers do not start with the Yoga exercises, they begin at the very moment that the door of the house of meditation closes behind us; for all the dangers of spiritual development are found in the seeker himself. Only in complete loneliness do we learn the true meaning of the words: know thyself! For only *then* do we stand before our own true

---

[1] Many examples of this, experienced by myself, will be cited in my next book *Bettler unter Toten* (Beggar amongst the Dead).

selves, not however, in looking at the distorted picture of the fight for survival in the world outside.

Nobody who has not experienced this himself can have an idea of the struggles of those who step into this entirely new world:

All lies fall away, deception ceases and only the need to vanquish or fall remains. Here there are no excuses for avoiding true enlightenment, no rosy pictures of consoling deception. Everyone must render an account of himself here, just as is usual at the moment of death; and just as there, our deceived psyche demands justice.

Then there will come the day of judgment, and he will know whether he will rise, or be thrown down pitilessly.

Those, however, who have come through will daily have a clearer horizon. Here they will find that their lonely days are full of sanctity and great peace, that they are not at all lonely as we understand it, that they carry a great inner happiness which does not ask for the fulfilment of desire. This happiness surpasses all other, because it is not that happiness whose reverse is unhappiness. It is not the happiness of fulfilled wishes, it is that of not wishing at all, of the not-needing-to-wish-any-more. From this point we can survey all the faculties of man. Here there are no more questions, for we know that there is no difference between question and answer, that there are no questions because there are no answers, that there is no answer because everything becomes part of the impenetrable circle of enlightenment. Those who know this do not ask, but also cannot answer.

It is for this reason that the ignorant goes past the enlightened after having asked him for the way. Those, however, who have understood, see all the answers in the eyes of the sage, feel close to him, and neither ask nor speak but know what lies *behind* empty words. Just as we pass millions of people and behind their tired, empty faces, we yet feel the depth of what was once their soul. We look for it but it is not there, and yet in depth and divine power it is incomparably greater than anything our confused senses may conceive.

There is no answer clearer than that of our inner voice. Let us learn to listen to it!

MEDITATION IN CHRISTIANITY

PROBABLY every Christian who has followed us so far will have wondered time and again:

How does all this relate to my own religious concepts?

Since meditation is by no means alien to Christianity, he is justified in asking why the subject was not related to Christian experience. Indeed, he might have learnt and profited much more had we done so, for to Western man the richest experiences and the greatest inner depth appear to be derived from Christianity.

If I followed a different course, *in spite of* it all, I did so for a very good reason which I shall now make clear. In order to make my explanation more convincing I shall endeavour to show what meditation meant to early Christianity, and what it means to the Christian of today.

As all religions in the world, Christianity, too, can be divided into two spiritual spheres: the prophetic and the mystical. There is no clear division of these spheres; but amongst the great religious men in particular, there is a clear division between God-awareness of prophetic and of mystical origin, so that the title "division of spheres" is not altogether inapplicable.

The basic element of prophetic piousness is faith. This is not a form of intellectual believing, but rather a confident, fundamental life-positive feeling of unconditional confidence.

Faith, confidence, and trust are the basic pillars of prophetic Christianity.

The God of the prophet has human traits, he is anthropomorphic—a spirit it is true, but full of primal force, full of life. He is the eternal God of the Fathers.

Mysticism is diametrically opposed to this prophetic feeling of life, and for it the basic element is the *experience* of God. Mysticism created the passive type as opposed to the active type of prophetic piousness.

Mysticism is that form of piousness in which "world and

the 'I' are radically denied" (Heiler).[1] The mystics' concept of God is a speculative interpretation of their own ecstatic experiences. "To the mystic, God is only the name given to his own experience" (Beck, Ecstasies 38). The God of biblical prophetic religion is not the immovable, infinite unity of the mystics, not resting stillness, but the living power of the will, activity. Not highest being (*summe esse*), but highest life (*summe vivere*) (Augustinus). He is Jahwe (JHVH), the revenging God, who not only demands childish but even slavish fear (Loyola), "before whose rage the earth trembles" (Jeremia), "a revenger and full of wrath" (Nahum).

The God of mysticism is "a non-God, a non-spirit, a non-person" (Master Eckhart). He is "beyond activity" (Plotinus), "still and stilling all" (Bernhard of Clairvaux), "a still being" (Tersteegen). As we can see: a static but not a dynamic God. And correspondingly, the religious life of these spheres is completely different: introvert in mysticism, extravert in prophetic religion.

In prophetic piousness prayer dominates, as we know from Luther: "Stand by me, do, you must do it!" Thus he prayed in Worms, and he explained this form of prayer:

"We must be shameless beggars, wanton and untiring."

How short a step it is from here to the most moving prayer of all religions: "My God, My God, why has thou forsaken me?"

The prayers of mystics are quite different. Master Eckhart said:

"We must pray so forcefully that all the limbs of Man and his strength, his eyes and ears, heart, mouth and all senses are in the prayer, and we may not stop till we find that we wish to become as one with what we have and pray for at that very moment, and that is God."

And Angelus Silesius sings:

"*No nobler prayer is, than worshipping we feel*
How we ourselves become, that before which we kneel."

In prophetic Christianity petitional prayers predominate, in mysticism prayers of praise: in the former, prayers for

[1] Heiler: *Das Gebet* (Prayer).

moral improvement, in the latter, for a *unio mystica*, a mystic unification with God, the *summum bonum*.

These brief remarks show what a prominent position prayer plays in all Christian religions. Indeed, we should not exaggerate if we said: the root of true Christianity lies in prayer. Yet it is not prayer itself which changes us, but the *basic attitude* on which we base our prayer: prophetic-biblical or mystic. Ed. von Hartmann said:

"The dialogue form (of prayer) is entirely dependent upon the duality of the persons in religious relationship. As soon as grace is recognized as the only true principle of salvation, as immanent grace, or the real unity with the absolute and, at the same time, impersonal God, this dialogue (of the process of salvation) becomes a monologue, i.e. prayer becomes self-communion and self-discussion. . . . Thus the truth of prayer lies in the absorption of the religious consciousness in itself, where God is neither known as Thou or as I, but as the absolute spiritual basis, the immanent purpose and holy power of one's own personal spiritual life" ("Religion of the Spirit").

In prayer we find an unexcelled interpretation of Christian meditation, for the prayer of the mystic *is* meditation.

The portals of the senses become closed (*myein*), so that we may "incline entirely towards the inside, to dip into the deep places of the soul" (Heiler), "to take ourselves back into ourselves" (Albertus Magnus).

"But it is not enough for the pious person, hungry for salvation, to free himself from the outer world of objects, rather must he free himself from his own Ego, from all selfish desire and demands. He must suppress those natural spiritual currents which create restlessness in man, and especially the stormy effects and the urgency of the Will, he must banish from his soul the colourful phantasies constantly rising from the depths of the emotions and passions; indeed, he must even abandon all thinking and evaluation of profane objects" (Heiler).

"The senses become blind" (Mechthild von Magdeburg), man "falls away from himself and from all things" (Seuse).

But this "unbecoming" (Eckhart) does not stem from the usual state of wakefulness, but from *above* it, from "super-conscious states of consciousness" (Heiler).

Just like meditation proper, deepest prayer can be divided into degrees of depth. Evidence for this is offered by the so-called prayer scales of Christian mystics.

The first step to meditative prayer is oral prayer which still lies outside the actual "prayer scale" (Joh. Arndt), it is the word without deeper soul responses, an introduction, so to speak.

The actual prayer scale always begins with conscious and deliberate concentration, with direct or indirect attention to God directly, the "self-recollection" (Joh. von Kreuz).

Those psychological explanations of Buddhist scholasticism, mentioned during our discussion of the spiritual processes in the different steps of meditation, are confirmed by Christian mystics—even if not quite so exhaustively and systematically. Their choice of words is often cruder, more original, more immediate, and also possibly, livelier and more plastic, for those not too closely acquainted with the subject.

On the first step of prayer—according to St. Theresa and other mystics—man himself is still active, while the spiritual states of higher prayer are created spontaneously. "Conscious concentration and meditation do not create these states spontaneously, but only prepare and favour the work of divine grace" (Heiler).

He who prays seeks solitude. By an act of the will he diverts his attention from the outer world, he "collects his senses and withdraws them from all seeing and hearing" (Guyon); "he frees himself from the distracting multiplicity of spiritual contents and suppresses the rush of emotions and ideas in his inner being" (Heiler). "Undisturbed by profane thought, he turns to things divine" (Algazali). This form of contemplation is one of "reasoned conclusions and of brooding on reason" (Petrus of Alcantara), "reasoned contemplation and reflection" (Joh. von Kreuz). St. Theresa, however, recommends "not to tire oneself by constantly new considerations" but "to let the activity of reason rest and to enter briskly into the presence of the Lord".

On the second step, the attentiveness characteristic of the first step disappears; discursive thought activity fades, "the lively play of concrete phantasy ceases, and all becomes very still in the soul of the contemplative" (Heiler). "Deeply contented, the soul rests in God; who grants it an inexplicable, sweet, peaceful happiness, who fills all its faculties with the deepest satisfaction, with the purest feeling of pleasure" (Teresa di Jesu). "The soul stops thinking altogether, and creates peace in God" (Joh. von Kreuz).

In its psychological effects, this second step too, corresponds exactly to its description in Buddhist texts. However, while the Buddhist monk turns inward without any object, "the soul" as Joh. von Kreuz puts it "rests lovingly in God, and unites wondrously with him, in joy and veneration and with the omnipotence of love." Here, too, God remains the immutable.

The third step of prayer differs neither in kind nor in manner from the second, but only in intensity.

St. Theresa calls this condition the "slumber of the faculties of the soul". The "soul enjoys infinitely more happiness, delight and pleasure than before. It wants to stream out in praise of divine love. It only asks for God, no longer belongs to itself, but only to Him."

Here there is a difference between the experiences of mystics on the one hand, and that of the Buddhists and Quietists on the other. Not delight and pleasure are the significant moments here, but unshakable equanimity. Not spiritual delight, but the quiet happiness which is beyond joy and pleasure.

The most decisive is the fourth and the last step to which the name "prayer" can no longer be applied, and of which the mystic David von Augsburg said:

"Man and God now become one."

Madame de Guyon gives an excellent description of it:

"Reason becomes obscured, memory pales, the will loses all tension; even the slightest movement of the ego ceases to be. Desire, inclination, wishes, opposition, disinclination, all is gone, the soul enters the dark awe-full condition of mystical death by passing into a state of complete insensitivity; it has become indifferent towards the world, towards itself, towards God. It neither loves nor hates any longer; it neither suffers nor rejoices; it does neither good nor evil, it does nothing at all. The soul has nothing, wants nothing, is nothing, and is becoming annihilated."

In spite of their apparent similarity, here we have the

THE SECRET OF MEDITATION

significant difference between the Nirvana of the Buddhist and the "mystical death" of the Quietist: Nirvana is the last, the highest goal of all striving for salvation, it is the deliverance from the vicious circle of re-births, from the causal law of cause and effect. "Mystical death" however, precedes resurrection. It is the "stage of transition towards the blessed unification with God" (Heiler).

Wherein does this difference lie? In the degree of absorption!

We are on fairly safe ground if we say that the mystics (with few exceptions) have not managed to pass beyond the second step of prayer. What has been described as the third and fourth steps is merely the abstract development of this second step, in a manner known to us from the chapter on "Total Meditation". It is the unfolding of that fourth step which Buddhists can attain, in which there are no more active elements of the will at all, and which no longer represents a further intensification, but merely a purification.

Now we are in a position to state why we have preferred the Buddhist technique to that of the Christian mystics.

To the Asiatic, meditation is a means for perfecting his life, and in this respect it is useful for us, too. For the mystic it is something *exclusively* religious, and to this we find it very hard to reconcile our way of life and also that of Buddhism.

"Pure mysticism is extremely individualistic" (Heiler). It knows only "God and the soul" (Augustinus). "The pious soul must be so united with God, as if nothing but God and the soul itself existed" (Albertus Magnus).

Escape from life, disdain for life and the world are the highest principles of mysticism, but neither of modern Christianity nor of Buddhism, where we do not say:

"Plant fear of you into my heart, that I may flee the world according to your commandments, and that I may hate it and wisely protect myself from it. Do not let me err in their midst, O Christ." (Symeon the New Theologian.)

How different is this from the old Buddhist text: "Neither on distant mountains nor at the bottom of the deep sea can the guilty escape the bitter fruits of his misdeeds" (Dhammapada 127).

It is not possible to identify mysticism (no matter of what

religion) with Buddhism, however many common characteristics they may have.

Let us make a short and factual survey of religious mysticism, the better to be able to judge their significant
differences.

All religions—as far as we have been able to ascertain—
develop some meditative practices, all of which have common
psychological characteristics.

Out of Islam there arose the meditative sects of the Sufis
and the Dervishes. Greek Orthodox Christianity, which is so
very branched and interwoven, has innumerable mystico-
meditative sects. These form a phenomenon in themselves
because in them—by means of an unlimited transition into
Asiatic fields (with branches towards Lamaism on the one
hand, as towards the Shamanism of Siberian Mongolia on
the other)—so much was mixed and borrowed, that we may
almost speak of a white spot on the religious map.

The Chassidic sect of the Jews, as also certain sections of
the Parsic Fire-Cult of Zoroaster bear mystico-meditative
marks.

The original Chinese religion, the old Indian Vedantic, the
Babylonian, the Egyptian, the old American, the old Roman
and the Greek Homerian religions show very few, if any,
marks of meditative intensification. Here there still rules
Eudaemonist prayer and the cult of Gods.

Only in the full development of Hellenic culture, in the
religion of the Hebrew prophets, in Confucianism and in
Taoism, and in the epoch of the Upanishad do we find religion
turning towards ethics. The deeper and the more individual
these religions, the more stress is placed on moral values.
Thus, there is a general but independent religious orientation
from the outside towards the inside. We are justified in assuming
that meditation was born at the very moment that a change in
this orientation took place.

Today there is not a single religion which is not—at least
in *one* of its sects—built on meditation. Indeed, even those
secret societies which appear to the mass as irreligious, such as
Freemasons, Rosicrucians, Pansophists, Kabbalists, etc., all
have their definite meditative practices.

It appears an almost Herculean labour to compare these

innumerable schools of meditation amongst themselves, but if we do so, we shall learn to our surprise that the difference is purely external: while the contents of meditation (not the objects themselves, but their pictures and their assumed measure of relative reality) constantly change from religion to religion, and from one secret society to the next, and thus apparently differ from one another, their basic psychological orientation, both in respect of the way and the goal, is astonishingly uniform. All of them fully correspond in their religious respect to Christian mysticism, even if the immanent Being in them, such as the God-concept, differs more from one religion to the next, than within the two main religious tendencies (prophetic and mystical) of the same religion. This fact shows both how all-penetrating is the concept of God, and how relative such a concept is as long as it is postulated *a priori*.

Every form of mysticism assumes the concept of God, in spite of its alleged immanence. Indeed, without this absolute hypothesis it would lose its meaning. As long as a concept is assumed and meditated upon (not as an object, as Buddhists do, but as a subject, as mystics do), it is transferred in the very form in which it was created by consciousness, to the sub- and the unconscious. The result differs from the starting-point only in that the concept becomes a spiritual experience. This may still take place in practice and with good effect up to the second step.

It is the *self-created* God who is experienced, not the *absolute* God.

Meditation, as we have learnt it in this book, is neutral from the start, i.e. it has no conscious religious bias; but it ends with the deepest religious experience. Those who believe they will lose their God when beginning to meditate without Him, have never known Him. However, they may find Him in meditation when they have looked deeply enough into themselves. For, only when the immanence of God has been proved unconditionally in the course of mystical or meditative experience, does He become a truly experienced power.

No, we do not wish to seek the Divine in thought. We must consciously put aside the picture of God formed by reason, and merely learn to open our heart, to let the truly divine stream in without its becoming a "picture" of God, without its becoming a "false idol".

Had we, in this book, adhered strictly to the words of the mystics, we should have introduced a picture into meditation which, with its terrible force, would have prevented the delicate truth from being born.

The true mystics were admittedly above the *picture* of God; but they only achieved this when they became saints. Our times offer little ground for sanctity. Therefore, rather than cry for the moon, we must do the nearest at hand and fulfil the duties and the demands of the day. We do not wish to flee from the world and to despise it (as the Quietists do), but we do want to master it.

All strictly biblical Christians reject mysticism as un-Christian because it is removed from Nature and life, from the God of the prophets.

This reproach does not seem to be unjustified, when the mystical experience at its apparent peak changes from the mental into the sensual, as in the bridal mysticism of the Pietists[1] and in the Bhaktas of the Vedanta.

They seem to have a clear psychological justification, for an ill-considered suppression of all natural drives creates an artificial over-stimulation of our feelings which manifest themselves in the transformed behaviour of our senses. In this condition the "experience of God" becomes a pathological hallucination. This will always happen when the desire for salvation is removed from natural law.

The mystics would not think of using meditation for worldly purposes; indeed, they would be wholly opposed to it. In the Buddhist sense—which never and nowhere has anything to do with mysticism—it represents the fulfilment of the striving for salvation, for meditation only begins where world and life are recognized and valued—in our own consciousness.

Thus, it would be equally wrong to reproach this book for using an Immanence (in the Buddhist sense) instead of the immanent God (in the Christian sense). Nothing is used, and

[1] "Oh Lord, love me much and love me often and long; the more often you love me, the purer I become; the more violently you love me, the more beautiful I become; the longer you love me, the holier I become on Earth . . . Think of how you can fondle my pure soul in your lap, O bring it about O Lord, even on me. Let me be your sole bed companion" (Mechthild von Magdeburg).

nothing is assumed. For our goal is neither the Unio Mystica nor Nirvana, but clear self-enlightenment. He who has reached this will find the *summum bonum* for himself.

"All psychology is based on self-observation; even religious psychology cannot advise against it, although no religious psychology can be built on it. To do so, the religious experience of modern man is largely too unproductive, too poor in content, too analytic and too powerless. However, even if we are lacking in immediate and powerful living piety based on meditation and prayer, we have at least the germs and the beginnings of the true religious experience, and the memories of completely naïve expressions of piety, especially childhood and youthful memories. We must use these so that, by means of real or hypothetical repetition of these sensations, we may obtain an understanding of this naïve piety. Self-observation is an absolutely essential hypothesis of all true religious psychology. He who has never felt his own religious impulse will never be able to penetrate that world of religion which is so full of wonders and riddles." (Heiler.)

"This is the only way, O monks, to explain existence, to overcome sadness and grievances, to banish death and misery, to find the right path, to realize Nirvana—it is correct meditation. Everything points to this, and to this alone. Thus spoke the Enlightened. The monks rejoiced at his words." (Sutta-Pitaka.)